From the Ascension to the Kingdom

Prophecies of Jesus' Olivet Discourse

David C Westcott

WestBow
PRESS
A DIVISION OF THOMAS NELSON

WestBow Press books may be ordered through booksellers or by contacting:

WestBow Press
A Division of Thomas Nelson
1663 Liberty Drive
Bloomington, IN 47403
www.westbowpress.com
1-(866) 928-1240

Because of the dynamic nature of the Internet, any Web addresses or
links contained in this book may have changed since publication and
may no longer be valid. The views expressed in this work are solely those
of the author and do not necessarily reflect the views of the publisher,
and the publisher hereby disclaims any responsibility for them.

ISBN: 978-1-4497-0412-4 (sc)
ISBN: 978-1-4497-0473-5 (e)

Scripture taken from the New King James Version. Copyright 1979, 1980,
1982 by Thomas Nelson, inc. Used by permission. All rights reserved.

Library of Congress Control Number: 2010934084

Printed in the United States of America

WestBow Press rev. date: 9/28/2010

CONTENTS

CHAPTER 1
BACKGROUND

During the week of His Passion, the Lord Jesus Christ taught in the temple at Jerusalem during the daytime, and retired to the Mount of Olives in the evening (Luke 21: 37). After one such visit to the temple, Jesus sat on the Mount of Olives and presented to His closest disciples one of the most comprehensive prophetic disclosures recorded in Scripture. This disclosure outlines the interlude between Jesus' ascension and the establishment of His Eternal Kingdom. This teaching is referred to as the Olivet Discourse.

The Mount of Olives is actually a mountain ridge extending approximately two miles in length running north and south, parallel to, and east of the Kidron Valley. The central peak of the Mount of Olives is called Olivet.[1] The Mount of Olives is directly mentioned in two other New Testament passages. The first mention is in John 8:1, where Jesus taught in the temple and afterwards went to the Mount of Olives. Perhaps Jesus went to Bethany or Bethphage which

---

1   Merrill C. Tenney, gen. ed., <u>The Zondervan Pictorial Encyclopedia of the Bible</u> (Grand Rapids, Michigan: Zondervan Publishing House, 1976), IV, 299-302.

were both located just east of the summit of Olivet.[2] The second New Testament reference is found in the book of Acts. Jesus' disciples returned to Jerusalem from Olivet after His ascension (Acts 1:12). The angels who stood by at the ascension explained how Jesus would return (Acts 1:11). The Mount of Olives is also mentioned twice in the Old Testament. 2 Samuel 15:30 is a reference to David's flight from his son Absolom. The second reference gives more insight into the Olivet Discourse. Zechariah 14:1-4 speaks of the coming of the day of the Lord, when the Lord will stand on the Mount of Olives, after the city is taken, and the mountain will split in two, producing a very large valley.

The third day of the Passion Week[3], the day of the discourse, proved to be a trying day for both our Lord and His disciples. The Lord and His disciples spent most of that day in the holy city of Jerusalem. His disciples listened intently as their Master tactfully rebuked a challenge to His authority, emanating from Jerusalem's leading religious authorities, the chief priests and scribes (Matthew 21:23-22:14, Mark 11:27-12:12, and Luke 20:1-18). As the day progressed, the disciples also witnessed the insidious questions aimed at trapping Jesus in His own words (Matthew 22:15-46, Mark 12:13-37, and Luke 20: 20-44). Finally, when the Pharisees, Herodians, Sadducees, and scribes could not prevail against Him, and they dared not question Him any further (Matthew 22:46, Luke 21: 40), Jesus pronounced a harsh denunciation upon Jerusalem's hypocritical religious leadership (Matthew 23). Though Mark and Luke briefly mention this denunciation, Matthew alone gives a fuller

---

2   Ibid. , page 300

3   There are varying opinions as to the chronology of the Passion Week. This book will follow the chronology suggested by Alfred Edershiem, The Life and Times of Jesus the Messiah (Grand Rapids, Michigan: Wm. B. Eerdmans Publishing Co., 1962), II, 363-654.

account of this scathing rebuke, including Jesus' lament over the city of Jerusalem and her desolation:

> O Jerusalem, Jerusalem, the one who kills the prophets and stones those who are sent to her_ How often I wanted to gather your children together, as a hen gathers her chicks under her wings, but you were not willing_ See_ Your house is left to you desolate; for I say to you, you shall see Me no more till you say, 'Blessed is He who comes in the name of the Lord_' (Matthew: 23: 37-39)[4]

Jerusalem was, for the Jews, the holy city, the place where God was to be worshipped (John 4:20). Jewish pilgrims would travel far distances to worship in the city. According to the Mosaic Law, the males of Israel were to appear in the place which God had chosen three times a year (Deuteronomy 16:16). The temple in Jerusalem was, from its inception in the days of Solomon, God's central place of worship, as it replaced the tabernacle as the meeting place with God. The sacrifices that were made to God were made in the court of the temple and this was the week of the Passover.

Solomon's temple was the original temple. King David conceived the idea of building a dwelling place for God (2 Samuel 7:1-3), but the LORD told David that he would not build the house for God (1 Chronicles 17:4). Solomon, David's son, would build the house (1 Chronicles 17:11-12). During the days of Jeremiah the prophet, Solomon's temple became so revered by the people of Judah that they believed, in spite of their sinful condition, that Jerusalem was invincible because it was the dwelling place of the

---

4   The Holy Bible: New King James Version (Nashville, Tennessee: Thomas Nelson, Inc., 1982). In this book all citations from the Bible will be from the New King James Version.

temple (Jeremiah 7:1-11). They had misplaced their trust. They trusted in the temple of God instead of trusting in the God of the temple. The city and the temple were both destroyed by the Babylonians (Jeremiah 39:8, 52:12-14). For seventy years the temple lay in ruins while the remnant of Judah sojourned in a foreign land, dreaming of the day when the temple would be rebuilt.

In the first year of Cyrus king of Persia, Zerubbabel was granted a decree stating that he was to lead a contingent of Jewish captives back to Jerusalem to rebuild the house of the LORD (Ezra 3:11-13). During the sixth year of king Darius the reconstructed temple was completed and dedicated (Ezra 6:15-16). This new temple nowhere approached the splendor and majesty of Solomon's temple, but the Jewish people once again had a place to worship their God.

Jerusalem and the temple underwent siege no less than five times during the interval between its reconstruction and the days of Herod the Great. In the fifteenth year of Herod the Great's reign, Herod decided to rebuild the temple as a part of his building program.[5] This rebuilding, however, was more than a remodeling of Zerubbabel's temple. Herod's temple was considerably larger and much more elaborate than the reconstructed temple of Zerubbabel. The main structures were completed in eight years, but the work continued for approximately seventy more years.[6] This was the temple which was observed by the disciples on the day of the Olivet Discourse.

---

5   Flavius Josephus, The Wars of the Jews in The Works of Flavius Josephus, trans. by William Winston (New York: A. L. Burt Company, Publishers, n.d.), I, i, 1-6; vii, 1-7; xiii, 1-11; xviii, 1-5; and II, iii, 1; v, 3.

6   Thomas S. McCall and Zola Levitt, Satan in the Sanctuary (Chicago: Moody Press, 1973), pp. 70-71.

A few days prior to the Olivet Discourse, Jesus had ridden into Jerusalem in fulfillment of the Messianic predictions of the Old Testament prophets (Zechariah 9:9 and Psalm 118:26). Expectations of the Kingdom must have reigned foremost in the disciples' thoughts, as they watched Jesus ride toward the city amidst the hails of, "Blessed is He who comes in the name of the LORD_" (Matthew 21:9, Mark 11:9-10, and Luke 19:37-38). This proclamation is cited from Psalm 118:25-28, where it is used as a prayer for the restoration and renewal of Israel:

Save now [Hosanna], I pray, O Lord:
O Lord, I pray, send now prosperity.
Blessed *is* he who comes in the name
    of the Lord_
God *is* the Lord_
    And He has given us light;
Bind the sacrifices to the
    horns of the altar.
You *are* my God,
    and I will praise You;
    You are my God , I will exalt You.

Yet, not everyone in the crowd that day cried out in exaltation of Jesus. Luke explains that certain Pharisees cried out from the throng demanding that Jesus silence the multitudes (Luke 19:39). Even as Jesus approached Jerusalem on what has been referred to as the "triumphal entry," He understood that this would not be the triumphal entry awaited by his followers. He knew that, though the crowds praised Him outside the city gates, within the walls of the city He would not be received as King. Jesus foreknew the rejection which awaited Him. As He looked over the city, Jesus let out a heaving sigh of anguish, while predicting the fall of Jerusalem (Luke 19:41-44). The religious leaders of Jerusalem were about to willfully reject the Messiah, Who is King, promised by the Old Testament prophets.

The following day, Jesus and His disciples entered the temple area and drove out the merchants and money changers (Matthew 21:12, Mark 11:15, and Luke 19:45). Perhaps, as the disciples observed this cleansing, they were reminded of another visit to the temple where Jesus also cleansed the temple. Three years earlier, during the time of the Passover (John 2:13), Jesus entered the temple area and drove out the merchants and money changers with a whip of chords (John 2:15). On that occasion, Jesus' authority was challenged as it would be on the day of the Olivet Discourse. The Jews demanded a sign (John 2:18), to which Jesus responded, "Destroy this temple, and in three days I will raise it up" (John 2:19). Those who heard this understood Jesus to be referring to Herod's temple, but Jesus spoke of His own body (John 2:20). Even the disciples were without understanding concerning Jesus' words until after the resurrection (John 2:22).

The Mount of Olives, the city of Jerusalem, Herod's temple, the Passover, and the understanding of the disciples, all play a vital role in understanding Jesus' discourse to His disciples on Olivet, and not only to the disciples, but, in a broader sense, to those who read the discourse passages. The following is an outline of the Olivet Discourse:

THE OLIVET DISCOURSE
Matthew 24-25; Mark 13; Luke 21

I. The Setting
　　　(Matthew 24:1-3, Mark 13:1-4, and Luke 21:5-7)
　　A. The disciples' observation of the temple
　　　　(Matthew 24:1, and Mark 13:1)
　　B. Jesus' response
　　　　(Matthew 24:2, Mark 13:2, and Luke 21:5-6)
　　C. The disciples' question(s)
　　　　(Matthew 24:3, Mark13: 3-4, and Luke 21:7)
II. Warning of Deception for the Disciples
　　　(Matthew 24:4-6, Mark 13:5-7, and Luke 21:7)
III. General Signs of Coming Judgment
　　　(Matthew 24:7-8, Mark 13:8, and Luke 21:10-11)
IV. Warnings of Persecution for the Disciples
　　　(Matthew 24:9, Mark 13:9-13, and Luke 21:12-19)
　　A. An opportunity to spread the Gospel
　　　　(Mark 13:9-10, and Luke 21:12-13)
　　B. How to Handle Persecution
　　　　　(Mark 13:11, and Luke 21:14-15)
　　C. The Extent of the Persecution
　　　　(Matthew 24:9, Mark 13:12-13a, and Luke 21:16-19)
V. The Desolation of Jerusalem
　　　(Luke 21:20-24)
VI. General Warnings to the Many
　　　(Matthew 24:10-14, and Mark 13:13b)
VII. The Abomination of Desolation
　　　(Matthew 24:15-22, and Mark 13:14-20)
VIII. The Second Warning of Deception
　　　(Matthew 24:23-28, and Mark 13:21-23)
IX. Signs in Heaven and on Earth
　　　(Matthew 24:29, Mark 13:24-25, and Luke 21:25-26)
X. The Sign of the Son of Man

The following is a composite of the three Gospel accounts of the Olivet Discourse. This writer believes that a composite helps to understand the discourse as a whole. The wording for this harmonized composite has been taken directly from the New King James version of the Bible. The paragraphing and ordering of events, however, are strictly this writer's impression of how these things should be arranged. As the book progresses various composite accounts will be drawn from the whole.

THE OLIVET DISCOURSE
Matthew 24-25; Mark 13; Luke 21
The Setting

Then Jesus went out and departed from the temple, and His disciples came to show Him the buildings of the temple. As He went out of the temple, one of His disciples said to Him, "Teacher see what manner of stones and buildings *are here_*" (Matthew 24:1, Mark 13:1)

Then, as some spoke of the temple, how it was adorned with beautiful stones and donations, Jesus answered and said to them, "Do you not see these great buildings? I say unto you, *as for* these things which you see, the days will come in which not one stone shall be left here upon another, that shall not be thrown down." (Matthew 24:2, Mark 13:2, Luke 21:5-6)

Now as He sat on the Mount of Olives opposite the temple, the disciples came to Him privately, *and* Peter, James, John, and Andrew asked Him, "Teacher, tell us when will these things be? And what sign *will there be* when these things are about to take place? And what *will be* the sign of Your coming, and the end of the age, when all these things will be fulfilled?" (Matthew 24:3, Mark 13:3-4, Luke 21:7)

Warning of Deception for the Disciples

And then Jesus answered and said to them: Take heed that no one deceives you. For many will come in My name saying, "I am the Christ," and "The time has drawn near," and they will deceive many. Therefore do not go after them. But when you hear of wars and rumors of wars or commotions, see that you are not troubled; for all *these things* must come to pass first, but the end *will* not *come* immediately. The end is not yet. (Matthew 24: 4-6, Mark 13:5-7, Luke 21:8-9)

General Signs of Coming Judgment

Then He said to them, "For nation will rise against nation, and kingdom against kingdom, and there will be great earthquakes in various places, and there will be famines and pestilences with troubles, and there will be fearful sights and great signs from heaven. All these things are the beginning of sorrows." (Matthew 24: 7-8, Mark 13:8, Luke 21:10-11)

Warnings of Persecution for the Disciples

But before all these things, watch out for yourselves, [for] they will lay hands on you and persecute *you*, delivering *you* up to councils, and you will be beaten in the synagogues and delivered into prisons. And you will be brought before kings and rulers for My name's sake. But it will turn out for you as an occasion for testimony. And the gospel must first be preached to all nations. (Mark 13:9-10, Luke 21:12-13)

Therefore settle *it* in your hearts not to meditate beforehand on what you will answer, but when they arrest you and deliver you up, do not worry beforehand, or premeditate what you will speak. But whatever is given you in that hour, speak that; for it is not you who speak, but the Holy Spirit; for I will give you a mouth and wisdom which all your adversaries will not be able to contradict or resist. (Mark 13:11, Luke 21:14-15)

At that time they will deliver you to tribulation and kill you; for you will be betrayed even by parents and brothers, relatives and friends. Now brother will betray brother to death, and a father his child; and children will rise up against parents and cause them to be put to death; and they send *some* of you to *your* deaths. And you will be hated by all nations for My name's sake. Yet not a hair of your head shall be lost. In your patience possess your souls. (Matthew 24:9, Mark 13:12-13, Luke 21:16-19)

The Desolation of Jerusalem

But when you see Jerusalem surrounded by armies, then know that its desolation is near. Then let those in Judea flee to the mountains, let those who are in the midst of her depart, and let not those who are in the country enter her. For these are the days of vengeance, that all things that are written may be fulfilled. But woe to those who are pregnant and those who are nursing babies in those days_ For there will be great distress in the land and wrath upon this people. And they will fall by the edge of the sword, and be led away captive into all nations. And Jerusalem will be trampled by the Gentiles until the times of the Gentiles are fulfilled. (Luke 21:20-24)

General Warnings to the Many

And then many will be offended, will betray one another, and will hate one another. Then many false prophets will rise up and deceive many. And because lawlessness will abound, the love of many will grow cold. But he who endures to the end shall be saved. And this gospel of the kingdom will be preached in the world as a witness to all the nations, and then the end will come. (Matthew 24:10-14, Mark 13:13b)

The Abomination of Desolation

Therefore when you see the "*abomination of desolation*," spoken of by Daniel the prophet, standing in the holy place, where it ought not (let whoever reads understand), then let those who are in Judea flee to the mountains. Let him who is on the housetop not go down into the house, [nor] enter to take anything out of his house. And let him who is in the field not go back to get his clothes. But woe to those who are pregnant and those who are nursing babies in those days. And pray that your flight may not be in winter or on the Sabbath. For then, *in* those days, there will be great tribulation such as has not been since the beginning of the creation of the world, which God created, until this time, no, nor ever shall be. And unless the Lord had shortened those days no flesh would be saved; but for the elect's sake, whom He chose, He shortened the days. (Matthew 24: 15-22, Mark 13: 14-20)

The Second Warning of Deception

Then if anyone says to you, "Look, here *is* the Christ_" or "Look, *He is* there_" do not believe *it*. For false christs and false prophets will arise and show signs and wonders, so as to deceive, if possible, even the elect. But take heed; see, I have told you all things beforehand. Therefore if they say to you, "Look, He is in the desert_" do not go out; or "Look, *He is* in the inner rooms_" do not believe *it*. For as lighting comes from the east and flashes in the west, so also will the coming of the Son of Man be. For wherever the carcass is, there the eagles will be gathered together. (Matthew 24: 23-28, Mark 13: 21-23)

Signs in Heaven and on Earth

But in those days, immediately after that tribulation, there will be signs in the sun, in the moon, and in the stars; the sun will be darkened, and the moon will not give its light; the stars will fall from heaven. And on the earth there will be distress of nations, with perplexity, the sea and the waves roaring; men's hearts failing them for fear and the expectation of those things which are coming on the earth, for the powers of the heavens will be shaken. (Matthew 24: 29, Mark 13: 24-25, Luke 21: 25-26)

The Sign of the Son of Man

Then the sign of the Son of Man will appear in heaven, and then all the tribes of the earth will mourn, and they will see the Son of Man coming on the clouds of heaven with power and great glory. Now when these things begin to happen, look up and lift up your heads, because your redemption draws near. And He will send His angels with a great sound of a trumpet, and they will gather together His elect from the four winds, from the farthest part of earth to the farthest part of heaven. (Matthew 24: 30-31, Mark 13:26-27, Luke 21: 27-28)

The Parable of the Fig Tree

Now learn this parable from the fig tree: Look at the fig tree and all the trees. When its branch has already become tender and puts forth leaves; *and* when they are already budding, you see and know for yourselves that summer is now near. So you also, when you see these things happening know that the kingdom of God is near, at the *very* doors. Assuredly, I say to you, this generation will by no means pass away until all these things are fulfilled. Heaven and earth will pass away, but my words will by no means pass away. (Matthew 24: 32-35, Mark 13:28-31, Luke 21: 29-33)

Judgment for Israel

But of that day and that hour no one knows, no, not even the angels, nor the Son, but My Father only. But as the days of Noah *were*, so also will the coming of the Son of Man be. For as in the days before the flood, they were eating and drinking, marrying and giving in marriage, until the flood came and took them all away, so also will the coming of the Son of Man be. Then two *men* will be in the field: one will be taken and the other left. Two *women will* be grinding at the mill: one will be taken and the other left. Watch therefore, for you do not know what hour our Lord is coming. Take heed, watch and pray; for you do not know when the time is. (Matthew 24:36-42, Mark 13: 32-33)

Parables of Readiness

But know this, that if the master of the house had known what hour the thief would come, he would have watched and not allowed his house to be broken into. Therefore you also be ready, for the Son of Man is coming at an hour when you do not expect Him. (Matthew 24:43-44)

It is like a man going to a far country, who left his house and gave authority to his servants, and to each his work, and commanded the doorkeeper to watch. Watch therefore, for you do not know when then master of the house is coming--in the evening, at midnight, at the crowing of the rooster, or in the morning--lest, coming suddenly, he find you sleeping. And what I say to you, I say to all: Watch_ (Mark 13:34-37)

Who is a faithful and wise servant, whom his master made ruler over his household, to give food in due season? Blessed is that servant whom his master, when he comes, will find so doing. Assuredly, I say unto you that he will make him ruler over all his goods. But if that evil servant says in his heart, "My master is delaying his coming," and begins to beat his fellow servants, and to eat and drink with drunkards, the master of that servant will come on a day when he is not looking for him and at an hour that he is not aware of, and will cut him in two and appoint him his portion with the hypocrites. There shall be weeping and gnashing of teeth. (Matthew 24:45-51)

But take heed to yourselves, lest your hearts be weighed down with carousing, drunkenness, and cares of this life, and that Day come on you unexpectedly. For it will come as a snare on all those who dwell on the face of the whole earth. Watch, therefore, and pray that you may be counted worthy to escape all these things that will come to pass, and to stand before the Son of Man. (Luke 21:34-36)

Then the kingdom of heaven shall be likened to ten virgins who took their lamps and went out to meet the bridegroom. Now five of them were wise, and five were foolish. Those who were foolish took their lamps and took no oil with them, but the wise took oil in their vessels with their lamps. But while the bridegroom was delayed, they all slumbered and slept. And at midnight a cry was heard: "Behold the bridegroom is coming; go out and meet him_" Then all those virgins arose and trimmed their lamps. And the foolish said to the wise, "Give us some of your oil, for our lamps are going out." But the wise answered saying, "No, lest there should not be enough for us and you; but go rather to those who sell, and buy for yourselves." And while they went to buy, the bridegroom came, and those who were ready went in with him to the wedding; and the door was shut. Afterward the other virgins came also saying, "Lord, lord open to us_" But he answered and said, "Assuredly I say to you, I do not know you." Watch therefore, for you know neither the day nor the hour in which the Son of Man is coming. (Matthew 25: 1-13)

For the kingdom of heaven is like a man traveling to a far country, who called his own servants and delivered his goods to them. And to one he gave five talents, to another two, and to another one, to each according to his own ability; and immediately he went on a journey. Then he who had received the five talents went and traded them, and made another five talents. And likewise he who received two gained two more also. But he who had received one went and dug in the ground, and hid his lord's money. (Matthew 25:14-18)

After a long time the lord of those servants came and settled accounts with them. So he who had received five talents came and brought five other talents, saying, "Lord you delivered to me five talents; look, I have gained five more talents besides them." His lord said to him, "Well done, good and faithful servant; you were faithful over a few things, I will make you ruler over many things. Enter into the joy of your lord." (Matthew 25:19-21)

He also who had received two talents came and said, "Lord, you delivered to me two talents; look, I have gained two more talents besides them." His lord said to him, "Well done, good and faithful servant: you have been faithful over a few things, I will make you ruler over many things. Enter into the joy of your lord." (Matthew 25:22-23)

Then he who had received the one talent came and said, "Lord, I knew you to be a hard man, reaping where you have not sown, and gathering where you have not scattered seed. And I was afraid, and went out and hid your talent in the ground. Look, there you have what is yours." But the Lord answered and said to him, "You wicked and lazy servant, you knew that I reap where I have not sown, and gather where I did not scatter seed. Therefore you ought to have deposited my money with the bankers, and at my coming I would have received back my own with interest. Therefore take the talent from him and give it to him who has ten talents. For to everyone who has, more will be given, and he will have abundance; but from him who does not have, even what he has will be taken away. And cast the unprofitable servant into outer darkness. There will be weeping and gnashing of teeth." (Matthew 25: 24-30)

The Judgment of the Gentiles

When the Son of man comes in His glory, and all the angels with Him, then He will sit on the throne of His glory. All the nations will be gathered before Him, and He will separate them one from another, as a shepherd divides his sheep from the goats. And He will set the sheep on His right hand, but the goats on the left. (Matthew 25:31-33)

Then the King will say to those on His right hand, "Come, you blessed of My Father, inherit the kingdom prepared for you from the foundation o the world: for I was hungry and you gave Me food; I was thirsty and you gave Me drink; I was a stranger and you took Me in; I was naked and you clothed Me; I was sick and you visited Me; I was in prison and you came to Me." Then the righteous will answer Him saying, "Lord, when did we see You hungry and feed You, or thirsty and give You drink? When did we see You a stranger and take You in, or naked and clothe You? Or when did we see you sick, or in prison, and come to you?" And the King will answer and say to them, "Assuredly, I say to you, inasmuch as you did it to one of the least of these My brethren, you did it to Me." (Matthew 25:34-40)

Then He will also say to those on the left hand, "Depart from Me, you cursed, into the everlasting fire prepared for the devil and his angels: for I was hungry and you gave Me no food; I was thirsty and you gave Me no drink; I was a stranger and you did not take Me in, naked and you did not clothe Me, sick and in prison and you did not visit Me." Then they will answer Him, saying, "Lord, when did we see you hungry or thirsty or a stranger or naked or sick or in prison, and did not minister to You?" Then He will answer them, saying, "Assuredly, I say to you, inasmuch as you did not do it to the least of these, you did not it to Me." And these will go into everlasting punishment, but the righteous into eternal life. (Matthew 25: 41-46)

CHAPTER 2
THE SETTING

There should be little doubt that Jesus' disciples were anticipating the arrival of the Kingdom of God. At least five of the disciples had followed Jesus from a time shortly after the inception of Jesus' earthly ministry (John 1:35 - 2:2) and the twelve closest disciples were specifically chosen to minister with Him about one year later (Mark 3:13-19). The twelve apostles, as they were later called, had walked closely with Jesus for a time span of between two or three years prior to the presentation of the Olivet Discourse.[1] During that time they had heard much with regard to the Kingdom.

From the outset of Jesus' public ministry, His message was that, for those who would listen, they should prepare for the coming of the Kingdom of Heaven (Matthew 4:17). The mighty works which Jesus had performed served to authenticate His message by foreshadowing the conditions which will be present during the Kingdom Age (Isaiah 61:1-

---

1   Ray E. Baughman, <u>The Life of Christ Visualized</u> (Mesquite, Texas: Shepherd Press, 1968), pp. 26, 50.

3). Later, when Jesus sent out the twelve to minister, He commissioned them to preach the very same message, the gospel of the Kingdom (Matthew 10:5-7, Luke 9:2). They, too, authenticated the message by signs and wonders which had been employed by Jesus (Matthew 10:8, Mark 6:7, and Luke 9:1). The Sermon on the Mount (Matthew 5-7), the parables of Matthew 13, and Jesus' private instructions to His disciples on greatness (Matthew 18), all centered on the Kingdom. Even the parables Jesus used on the day of the discourse were about the Kingdom of God (Matthew 21:31,43; 22:2). Whatever else the disciples may have been contemplating as they ascended Olivet on that Tuesday afternoon, most certainly their minds were occupied with the coming of Jesus' Kingdom.

Keeping in mind that the disciples eagerly anticipated the establishment of the Kingdom, the Olivet discourse begins with Jesus and His disciples exiting the temple for the long walk across the Kidron Valley and up the slope of Olivet. As they walked the following unfolded:

> Then Jesus went out and departed from the temple, and His disciples came to show Him the buildings of the temple. As He went out of the temple, one of His disciples said to Him, "Teacher see what manner of stones and buildings *are here_*" (Matthew 24:1, Mark 13:1)

Perhaps the excitement of the Passover week prompted the disciples to take notice of the buildings of the city. Maybe Jesus' declaration of the desolation of the city caused the disciples to focus on the structures within the city.[2] Whatever

---

2 Alfred Edershiem, <u>The Life and Times of Jesus the Messiah</u> (Grand Rapids, Michigan: Wm. B. Eerdmans Publishing Company, 1962), II, 432-433.

drew the disciples' attention to the buildings, they probably weren't ready for Jesus' response:

> Then, as some spoke of the temple, how it was adorned with beautiful stones and donations, Jesus answered and said to them, "Do you not see these great buildings? I say unto you, *as for* these things which you see, the days will come in which not one stone shall be left here upon another, that shall not be thrown down." (Matthew 24:2, Mark 13:2, Luke 21:5-6)

Jesus had not only predicted the desolation of Jerusalem, but also predicted the destruction of the temple. In addition to these two predictions, Jesus intimated that He was going away, when He said, "… you shall see Me no more till you say, 'blessed is He comes in the name of the LORD_'" (Matthew 23:39). These things lead the disciples to question Jesus:

> Now as He sat on the Mount of Olives opposite the temple, the disciples came to Him privately, *and* Peter, James, John, and Andrew asked Him, "Teacher, tell us when will these things be? And what sign *will there be* when these things are about to take place? And what *will be* the sign of Your coming, and the end of the age, when all these things will be fulfilled?" (Matthew 24:3, Mark 13:3-4, Luke 21:7)

Outwardly there appear to be three questions being asked by the disciples: 1. When will these things be? [most likely a question with regard to the desolation of Jerusalem and the destruction of the temple] 2. What sign shall precede these things? and 3. What sign will announce Your return and the end of the age? However the final phrase of the inquiries, "… when all these things will be fulfilled," seems to tie these questions into one distinct question. For the disciples the desolation of Jerusalem, the destruction of the temple, the second coming of Jesus, and the end of the age are understood to be all tied into one event. Stanley Toussaint, Th. D., explains the disciples' perception of future events as follows:

> In their minds they had developed a chronology of events in the following sequence: (1) the departure of the King, (2) after a period of time the destruction of Jerusalem, and (3) immediately after Jerusalem's devastation the presence of the Messiah.[3]

If one could express the intent of the disciples' questions in a single thought , it might possibly read, "When and how will the Kingdom come?" G. Campbell Morgan expresses the relationship of the disciples' questions as follows:

> Evidently in their minds they [the disciples] associated three things: the destruction of the Temple, the presence of Jesus, and the ending of the age. … they had some conception of a purpose of God, which was working out toward a consummation. They were looking for the setting up of a material Kingdom.[4]

Whether one sees three questions or one question, the question(s) center around this single thought. Therefore, the reader of the discourse must keep in mind the fact that Christ's audience consisted of His disciples, who represented Old Testament saints awaiting the coming Kingdom.

When Jesus sighed out the lament, "for I say to you, you shall see Me no more till you say, 'Blessed is He who

---

3 Stanley Toussaint, "The Argument of Matthew" (Th. D. dissertation, Dallas Theological Seminary, 1957), pp. 315-316.

4 G. Campbell Morgan, *Matthew* in <u>Studies in the Four Gospels</u> (Westwood, New Jersey: Fleming H. Revell Company, 1931), I, 281.

comes in the name of the LORD_'" (Matthew 23:39), many who stood by must have understood the prophetic significance of such a statement. In the days of Moses, God had promised that the children of Israel would experience both blessing and cursing through the covenant which He was making with them, the Mosaic Covenant. But, He also promised that after both the blessing and cursing had been experienced, there would come a time for restoration. Since the Mosaic Covenant was conditional. the restoration would also be conditional. The condition for restoration would be that the nation must first return to the Lord their God (Deuteronomy 30:1-10). Later, as the nation was about to experience the full extent of the curse, God used the prophet Jeremiah to announce a New Covenant, an unconditional covenant, which would accompany the restoration of the reunited nations of Israel and Judah (Jeremiah 31:31-34). Other Old Testament prophets wrote, with regard to this New Covenant, that it would establish a new age, an age of peace and prosperity for the nation of Israel and for the world (Isaiah 55:3, 65:17-25; Jeremiah 32:40-44; Ezekiel 34:25-31, and 36:25-30). Some of the provisions of the New Covenant link it to another covenant made between God and the nation of Israel, the Davidic Covenant, with its promise of an everlasting Kingdom (Isaiah 55:3; Jeremiah 33:14-15; and 2 Samuel 7:8-16). Therefore, to the Jewish mind, during the days of Jesus' earthly ministry, there were but two ages, the present corrupt age and the coming age, the Kingdom age.

The Upper Room Discourse (John 13-17), which takes place after the Olivet Discourse, attests to the fact that when Jesus spoke of His departure, His disciples were unaware of where He was going. Jesus had told His disciples that He was going away, and that where He was going they would not be able to immediately follow. To this statement both

Peter and Thomas responded by asking Him where He was going (John 13:36, 14:5), and they apparently represented the sentiments of the eleven. Though Jesus told them that He was going to Jerusalem, and that He would be put to death there, somehow they managed to pass His words off as one of the hard sayings which they could not understand (John 16:16-18). While the disciples listened to Jesus on the slope of Olivet, their thoughts were far from being involved in His upcoming death. So much so that they had avoided any thought of His dying.

The disciples hadn't yet grasped the idea that Jesus was going to be crucified, resurrected, and ascended into heaven until His return to establish His Kingdom. They had no conception of a Church age which would exist between His departure and His return. They were awaiting an immediate establishment of the Kingdom. Jesus knew and therefore formulated His reply around both the things which the disciples understood and their misunderstandings.

This chapter has set the stage for Jesus' discourse. The disciples were expecting a simple answer to their inquiries, but Jesus was about to give them a much more complex reply to their questions. The next chapter is where Jesus begins His response to the matter of the end times.

CHAPTER 3
THE WARNING

Jesus was aware of the disciples' expectation that the Kingdom would come soon. Looking back at the previous chapter, in the minds of the disciples there were but two things necessary for the establishment of the Kingdom: 1. the desolation of Jerusalem, including the destruction of the temple, and 2. the second coming of Jesus.[1] Jesus understood that the disciples could easily be led astray by the possibilities of these two events.

All three synoptic gospel accounts open the same words of warning. Most likely these are the actual opening words of the discourse which Jesus presented:

> Take heed that no one deceives you. For many will come in My name saying, "I am the Christ," and "The time has drawn near," and they will deceive many. Therefore do not go after them. But when you hear of wars and rumors of wars or commotions, see that you are not troubled; for all *these things*

---

1   Stanley Toussaint, "The Argument of Matthew" (Th. D. dissertation, Dallas Theological Seminary, 1957), pp. 315-316.

must come to pass first, but the end *will* not *come* immediately. The end is not yet. (Matthew 24: 4-6, Mark 13:5-7, Luke 21:8-9)

Jesus was clearly directly addressing His disciples as He began this teaching. The opening words are, "Take heed that no one deceives you." The personal pronoun "you" speaks of His audience, the disciples.

The expression "in my name" is of significance in this warning. Kenneth Wuest has the following to state about the phrase:

> The phrase "in my name" is literally, "upon the basis of my name," thus, "basing their claims on the use of my name." The name "Christ," namely, "Messiah," was a title with which to conjure, for Israel was looking for its Messiah. [2]

The times were ripe for false messiahs. The tensions between Rome and the Jews were mounting and many Jews were looking for a political deliverer. At one point in Jesus' ministry, after the feeding of the five thousand, some Jews had even desired to forcibly make Jesus their king. Jesus perceived their intent and went off by Himself onto a mountain (John 6:15). The Jews were ready to receive anyone who claimed to be their Messiah, so long as he promised deliverance from the Roman tyranny. Jesus understood that such false messiahs would arise after His departure, and it was important that the disciples understood this as well. They would have much with which to be concerned, without being caught up by rumors of Christ's return.

While it is true that false messiahs will arise during the tribulation period, particularly the Antichrist himself, this

---

2   Kenneth S. Wuest, <u>Mark in the Greek New Testament for the English Reader</u> (Grand Rapids: Wm B Eerdman Publishing Co., 1950) p.245.

portion of the discourse is directed at the false christs of the period of the early disciples. A similar set of warnings appears later in the discourse, and is presented in conjunction with tribulation prophecies (Matthew 24:23-28, Mark 13:21-23). These warnings parallel each other, but are directed toward separate recipients.

Having warned the disciples with regard to false christs, Jesus, next, told them not to be troubled by wars and rumors of wars. At first glance, this statement would seem to be out of place, since the disciples had not mentioned wars in their inquiries. However, they did ask about "these things." From the context of the passage, "these things" would seem to be in reference to Jesus' predictions of Jerusalem's desolation, His departure, and the destruction of the temple. Now, the destruction of the temple was described in such a way as to discount a natural disaster as the cause for its dismantling. The most likely explanation for a stone by stone dismantling would have been that it would be the work of an army, suggesting a war. There may have been some discussion of this sort among the disciples as the made the climb to the place on Olivet where they rested. The Scripture doesn't tell us much about what was said along the road, or even whether there was any discussion, other than the disciples' admiration of the buildings of the city.

Another possible reason for the mention of wars and rumors of wars has to do with the Old Testament prophecy of Daniel in chapter nine. In that chapter Daniel was told about the seventy weeks, literally seventy sevens, which would complete the restoration of the nation of Israel. The end of Daniel 9:26 states that "... till the end of the war desolations are determined." This may have been something which the disciples had discussed with Jesus as they spoke about the coming Kingdom. Whatever the case, the disciples apparently had good reason for associating the end of the age with a war.

Jesus and His disciples were aware that the political climate of their day was such that a war could erupt at any moment. The years leading up to Jerusalem's destruction in A.D. 70 were marked by wars and rumors of war which struck terror in the hearts of many Jews. Flavius Josephus, a noted Jewish historian of the first century, attested to these conditions by writing,

> Now as for the Jews, some of them could not believe the stories that spoke of war; but those that did believe were in the utmost distress how to defend themselves, and the terror diffused itself presently through them all, for the army was already come to Ptolemais.[3]

Jesus forewarned His disciples with regard to these things, so that they would not be overwhelmed by these disturbances as other Jews would be. Being forewarned and realizing that the end would not come immediately, the disciples would be able to focus on other more important eventualities, and so avoid being troubled by them.

Jesus was aware of the eagerness of the disciples toward the establishment of the Kingdom. In their inquiries the disciples had lumped the destruction of the temple, Jesus' return, and the end of the age into one package. They were ready for all of it to happen at once. Therefore, Jesus, without giving a definite time frame for the coming of the end of the age, specified that it would not happen immediately. By doing so, He was setting up a distinction between that which would come to Jerusalem in 70 A.D. and the end

---

3   Flavius Josephus, The Wars of the Jews in The Works of Flavius Josephus, trans. by William Whiston (New York: A.L. Burt Company, n.d.), II, x, 1.

of the age. Charles Spurgeon has aptly made this point by stating,

> The destruction of Jerusalem was the beginning of the end, the great type and anticipation of all that shall take place when Christ shall stand at the latter day upon the earth. It was *an* end, but not *the* end: "the end is not yet." [4]

Oddly enough, even today, when wars and rumors of wars are mentioned, much discussion is raised concerning Christ's return. Jesus, however, counseled His disciples to not be troubled by these things. There will be wars and rumors of war when the end approaches, but these are not the signal for the end of the age. As Jesus put it, "… the end will not come immediately. The end is not yet." In fact, the apostle Paul, in his first letter to the Thessalonians, describes the conditions prior to the day of the Lord by stating, "For when they say 'Peace and safety_' then sudden destruction comes upon them, as the labor pains upon a pregnant woman" (I Thessalonians 5:3). The day of the Lord is coming at a time when the world is not looking for it, but, as Christians, we are to be continually on watch.

The next chapter will delve into the reasons why the end will not come immediately. They deal with things which have been signs for coming judgment. Yet, even these things are not the signs of the end of the age.

---

4 C.H. Spurgeon, The Gospel of the Kingdom (Pasadena, Texas: Pilgrim Publications, 1974), p. 213.

CHAPTER 4
GENERAL SIGNS OF COMING JUDGMENT

In the previous chapter Jesus warned the disciples about false messiahs and exhorted them not to be troubled by wars and rumors of wars. Jesus went on to explain why they should not look to wars and rumors of wars as the signal for the end of the age. The following is His explanation:

> Then He said to them, "For nation will rise against nation, and kingdom against kingdom, and there will be great earthquakes in various places, and there will be famines and pestilences with troubles, and there will be fearful sights and great signs from heaven. All these things are the beginning of sorrows." (Matthew 24: 7-8, Mark 13:8, Luke 21:10-11)

The Old Testament foretold of terrible judgment, which would come upon the face of the earth prior to the restoration of the kingdom. The prophet Jeremiah referred to this judgment as "the time of Jacob's trouble" (Jeremiah 30:7). Daniel referred to the same judgment as a "... time of trouble, such as never was since there was a nation, *even* to that same time: …" (Daniel 12:1). The natural thing to do, then, would be to look for signs that would indicate that such a judgment was about to occur as an indication of the approach of the end of the age. In a sense, such judgments are an indication of the coming of the end. They all serve as precursors and patterns of the judgment which shall take place in the day of the Lord.

Wars, earthquakes, famines, pestilences, and disturbances in the heavens have been signs of judgment for the nation of Israel in times past. Yet Jesus assured His disciples that these were not the signs for which they sought. These are only the "beginning of sorrows" (Matthew 24:8; Mark 13:8). The word "sorrows" literally means "the pains of childbirth."[1] Just as the pains of childbirth intensify as the moment of delivery approaches, even so these signs of judgment will increasingly worsen as the day of Israel's deliverance nears.

Historians have recorded countless wars, earthquakes, pestilences, and heavenly disturbances since the time of Christ's first coming. These things were prevalent in the days surrounding Jerusalem's destruction in A.D. 70, and they will be prevalent in the days of the great tribulation. Alford registers five earthquakes which took place after the giving of this prophecy and before the demise of Jerusalem.[2] As with most wars, famine and pestilences followed the days of war in Palestine. Yet, Jesus was not speaking specifically of the events centered around Jerusalem's downfall, nor was He speaking directly to the judgments which will come during the great tribulation (Revelation 7:14), though both

---

1   Kenneth S. Wuest, <u>Mark in the Greek New Testament for the English Reader</u> (Grand Rapids: Wm. B Eerdman Publishing Co., 1950), p. 246.

2   Henry Alford, <u>The Greek Testament</u>, revised by Everett F. Harrison (Chicago: Moody Press, 1958), I, 236-237.

periods have been and will be marked by such judgments. John Walvoord states,

> In general these signs have been partially fulfilled in the present age and have characterized the period between the first and second coming of Christ. They should be understood as general signs rather than specific signs that the end in near.[3]

Ever since Jesus' crucifixion, the world has been in the end times (I Peter 1:20; I John 2:18). Therefore, the disciples were not to look to wars and rumors of wars as the signs of the end of the age, because these kinds of things "must come to pass first." These things are all indicators of the terrible judgment which will come to pass during the time of Jacob's trouble.

Over the centuries since the founding of the Church and even today, wars, earthquakes, pestilences, and heavenly disturbances have been and are prevalent. Some say that they have come with increasing intensity. Others say that they are only being reported more frequently giving an increasing awareness of these things. Whatever the case we know that the coming of Christ is drawing nearer and has been drawing nearer ever since the establishment of the Church in the first century. The presence of these signs serves to verify what Jesus told His disciples. There is no way of knowing how intense these signs will become before Christ's return. What is known is that Christ has more important matters for us to focus our attention upon.

A danger exists with becoming overly caught up in the signs of Christ's return. The apostle Paul addressed this danger in his second letter to the Thessalonians (II Thess. 2:2-4). In anticipating Christ's return, some have

---

3   John F. Walvoord, <u>Matthew: Thy Kingdom Come</u> (Chicago: Moody Press, 1974), pp. 183-184.

gone as far as stopping all normal activity, selling their goods, and isolating themselves from society. In doing so, they err, because what Christ expects at His return is that His followers be active with works He has given to them to do. There is also a danger of those caught up in the signs of Christ's return, becoming busybodies (II Thess. 3:11). Paul, on the other hand, admonished the early believers of Thessalonica to not become weary with doing good (II Thess. 3:13), and to stand fast and hold to the traditions which they had been taught (II Thess. 2:15).

CHAPTER 5
PERSECUTIONS

Jesus warned the disciples against seeking after false messiahs, and He admonished to not be troubled by wars and rumors of wars. He explained that nations would rise up against nation, and that there would be earthquakes and pestilences in various places, and that there would be heavenly disturbances. Yet, all of these things were not what the disciples were to focus their attention upon.

The disciples were going to face trials and persecutions, and they needed to understand that they would have to rely on the power of the Holy Spirit during those times. The following is what Jesus had to say to His disciples with regard to their upcoming trials:

> But before all these things, watch out for yourselves, [for] they will lay hands on you and persecute *you*, delivering *you* up to councils, and you will be beaten in the synagogues and delivered into prisons. And you will be brought before kings and rulers for My name's sake. But it will turn out for you as an occasion for testimony. And the gospel must first

be preached to all nations. (Mark 13:9-10, Luke 21:12-13)

Therefore settle *it* in your hearts not to meditate beforehand on what you will answer, but when they arrest you and deliver you up, do not worry beforehand, or premeditate what you will speak. But whatever is given you in that hour, speak that; for it is not you who speak, but the Holy Spirit; for I will give you a mouth and wisdom which all your adversaries will not be able to contradict or resist. (Mark 13:11, Luke 21:14-15)

At that time they will deliver you to tribulation and kill you; for you will be betrayed even by parents and brothers, relatives and friends. Now brother will betray brother to death, and a father his child; and children will rise up against parents and cause them to be put to death; and they send *some* of you to *your* deaths. And you will be hated by all nations for My name's sake. Yet not a hair of your head shall be lost. In your patience possess your souls. (Matthew 24:9, Mark 13:12-13, and Luke 21:16-19)

This warning has three parts to it. The first part forecasts the trials and tribulations through which the disciples and their disciples would go. The second part deals with how the disciples should respond under such circumstances. The third and final part tells the extent of these trials and tribulations.

Though the disciples were not to trouble themselves with wars, rumors of war, earthquakes, pestilences, or heavenly disturbances, Jesus explained to them that there were situations awaiting them which would be of much concern. Once again note that this portion of the discourse is directed particularly to Jesus' disciples. This fact is recognizable by the added use of the personal pronoun "you." Up to this point in the discourse, Jesus had been addressing general conditions which would have worldwide effects, and conditions which would affect the nation of Israel. Kenneth Wuest notes, "The pronoun is added here (Mark 13:9) for emphasis. It is, 'But, as for you, do not think only of what is coming on the Jewish nation and on the world, but also on yourselves.'"[1] The destruction of Jerusalem would be of grave concern to the nation of Israel, and the wars, earthquakes, famines, pestilences, and heavenly disturbances would be of worldwide concern, but the disciples were to take care for the trials, persecutions, and tribulations awaiting them personally. Though these other things would be of importance, Jesus demonstrated His compassion for His disciples by emphasizing these warnings concerning the troubles which they themselves would encounter.

The disciples of Jesus were eagerly anticipating the coming of a glorious Kingdom in which they would live and reign with their Lord. In the months prior to the Passion Week, Jesus' disciples showed their anticipation of their presence in the Kingdom by discussing among themselves such matters as who would be the greatest in the Kingdom, and what their reward would be for being Jesus' followers (Matthew 18:1, 19:27, 20:20-21; Mark 9:34, 10:35-35; Luke 9:46; etc.) They probably were not prepared for what Jesus would tell them at this point in the discourse. For He explained that they would be persecuted, beaten, thrown into prison, and tried before kings. This was quite a contrast to the picture they had drawn for themselves. Instead of telling them of the wonderful things they would experience when they entered the Kingdom, He was telling them of

---

1 Kenneth S. Wuest, <u>Mark in the Greek New Testament for the English Reader</u> (Grand Rapids: Wm B. Eerdman Publishing Co., 1950), p. 247

the things they must suffer in order to spread the good news of the Kingdom. Yet, later, when they would actually encounter these sufferings, there must have been a sense of reassurance as they recalled these words which the Master had spoken prior to His own sufferings.

Following the Day of Pentecost, during the very outset of the preaching of the gospel, the disciples began to experience trials and persecutions of the nature of those spoken of in the opening portion of this warning. Shortly after the healing of a lame man at the temple gate, Peter and John were placed into custody overnight because of their teaching and preaching to the people about Jesus' resurrection (Acts 4:1-3). The following day the two of them stood before the council in Jerusalem, testifying to the council about what Jesus had done (Acts 4: 5-20). As the gospel continued going out, all of the apostles together were arrested and placed into the common prison (Acts 5:17-21). As they were set before the council, they testified concerning Jesus (Acts 5:27-32). They were also beaten for speaking by the authority of Jesus, and rejoiced that they were counted worthy of suffering for their testimony of Christ (Acts 5: 40, 41). Later still, Stephen, one of the apostles' disciples, was accused of blasphemy and brought before the council (Acts 6: 8-15). He, too, testified of Jesus Christ before the council (Acts 7: 1-53). Peter was again imprisoned by Herod at a later date (Acts 12: 3-4). In fact the entire book of Acts itself appears to be a testimony to the acts of suffering by the apostles and their followers. Through all of this persecution, the gospel continued going forth and spread to the nations.

Jesus was also aware that, in light of these persecutions, the disciples might become anxious as how to defend themselves, especially when they were to be tried before governors and kings. These were for the most part unlearned men. Jesus assured them that He would give them wisdom and the words to speak when the time came for them to speak on His behalf. The apostle Paul has a bit of wisdom with regard to this matter:

> For you see your calling, brethren, that not many wise according to the flesh, not many mighty, not many noble, are called. But God has chosen the foolish things of the world to put to shame the things which are mighty; and the base things of the world and the things which are despised God has chosen, and the things that are not to bring to nothing the things that are, that no flesh should glory in His presence. But of Him you are in Christ Jesus, who became for us wisdom from God--and righteousness and sanctification and redemption-- that as it is written, 'He who glories let him glory in the Lord.' (I Corinthians 1:26-31)

Peter and John had no time to prepare an adequate defense (even if they had been capable of doing so on their own), but were called upon to speak before the Jewish council after healing the lame man, and the council marveled at their boldness, and was unable to accuse them of a punishable offense (Acts 4:13-14, 21-22). When Peter and John gave testimony before the council, their speech gave evidence to the fact that "they had been with Jesus" (Acts 4:13). The glory belongs to Jesus, but the privilege has been given to us to be used as His instruments in proclaiming a testimony to His glory.

Stephen was also full of wisdom, such that the Synagogue of Freedmen "were not able to resist the wisdom and the spirit by which he spoke" (Acts 6:10). The admonition to the disciples to settle the matter in their on hearts, in the second section of this warning, was given for their immediate benefit. Certainly there is application here to be drawn for the present and future generations, but the initial fulfillment of the prophecy in this portion of the discourse belongs to the generation of the disciples themselves.

Furthermore, Jesus went on to explain the extent to which such trials and persecutions would be carried out. This was not the first occasion on which Jesus had warned these disciples of the persecution awaiting them, Earlier in His ministry, when Jesus sent out the twelve apostles, He warned them that He was sending them out "as sheep in the midst of wolves" (Matthew 10:16). In the discourse which Jesus gave on that occasion, He warned, "A disciple is not above *his* teacher, nor a servant above his master" (Matthew 10:24). Coupled with this statement, Jesus exhorted the disciples not to worry about being physically killed, but to be concerned with spiritual death (Matthew 10:28). In giving the Olivet Discourse, Jesus knew that He was to be crucified in a few days, and He desired that His disciples be aware that they too would undergo great persecutions, even to the point of death.

Jesus emphasized, in light of all the treachery that would take place during the persecution and trials, some of the disciples themselves would be killed (Luke 21:16). There is little doubt that Jesus was speaking of His disciples' deaths. The first recorded martyr of the Church was Stephen (Acts 7: 59-60), but some time later the apostle James, one of the twelve, was killed by the sword at the hand of Herod the king (Acts 12: 1-2). According to John Fox, the apostle John "…was the only apostle who escaped a violent death."[2] Though John escaped violent death, he in no way escaped persecution (see Revelation 1:9). Such persecutions and martyrdom are present even today and will increase during

2   John Fox, <u>Fox's Book of Martyrs</u>, edited by William Byron Forbush (Philadelphia, Pa.: Universal Book and Bible House, 1926), p. 5.

the great tribulation, but its original fulfillment began in the first century.

In our affluent Western culture, the message of "suffering for Christ" is not one that appears to be popular. Yet Jesus told us that we could expect troubles as long as we are in the world. Jesus said,

> "These things I have spoken to you, that in Me you may have peace. In the world you will have tribulation; but be of good cheer, "I have overcome the world." (John 16: 33)

The apostle Peter also wrote on the trials that face us. He wrote,

> "Beloved, do not think it strange concerning the fiery trial which is to try you, as though some strange thing happened to you; but rejoice to the extent that you partake of Christ's sufferings, that when His glory is revealed, you may also be glad with exceeding joy." (I Peter 4:12-13)

Peter wasn't alone in recognizing the significance of suffering with Christ. The apostle Paul wrote the following to the Romans,

> "The Spirit Himself bears witness with our spirit that we are children of God, and if children, then heirs -- heirs of God and joint heirs with Christ, if indeed we suffer with *Him*, that we may also be glorified together.
>
> For I consider that the sufferings of this present time are not worthy *to be compared* with the glory which shall be revealed in us." (Romans 8: 16-18)

Suffering with Christ is not something to be dreaded, but something to be regarded as a privilege.

CHAPTER 6
THE DESOLATION OF JERUSALEM

Jesus warned His disciples of the events which were to come in their lifetimes. At this point in the discourse, Jesus answers the disciples' question, "Teacher, tell us when will these things be? And what sign will there be when these things are about to take place?" (Luke 21:7) Jesus directly approached the issue of Jerusalem's desolation and the destruction of the temple. The gospel of Luke is the only one of the three records to delineate this portion of the discourse. The following is Jesus' response to the question of the sign which would announce the demise of Jerusalem:

> But when you see Jerusalem surrounded by armies, then know that its desolation is near. Then let those in Judea flee to the mountains, let those who are in the midst of her depart, and let not those who are in the country enter her. For these are the days of vengeance, that all things that are written may be fulfilled. But woe to those who are pregnant and those who are nursing babies in those days_ For there will be great distress in the land and wrath

upon this people. And they will fall by the edge of
the sword, and be led away captive into all nations.
And Jerusalem will be trampled by the Gentiles
until the times of the Gentiles are fulfilled. (Luke
21:20-24)

Perhaps Matthew and Mark did not include this portion
of the discourse because, in an indirect manner, they had
already addressed this question. In the opening verse of the
discourse, the disciples were told not to be troubled by wars
and rumors of war, and that would include the war which
initiated the destruction of Jerusalem. Luke, however, was
the historian among the gospel writers, and this segment
would be significant from a historical point of view. Luke
was concerned with the events which would lead up to
the demise of Jerusalem (see Luke 19:4-44). Moreover, the
dating of the gospel of Luke suggests that he wrote this at a
time when these events were about to unfold.

Attempts have been made to link Luke's account of
Jerusalem's desolation with the accounts of Jacob's trouble
found in Matthew and Mark. The following is a comparison
chart of these two different events.

COMPARISON CHART

Jerusalem's fall (A.D. 70) Luke 21:20-24	Jacob's Trouble Matthew 24:15-22 and Mark 13: 14-20
THE SIGN: But when you see Jerusalem surrounded by armies, then know its desolation is near. (Luke 21: 20)	THE SIGN: Therefore when you see the *"abomination of desolation*," spoken of by Daniel the prophet, standing in the holy place, where it ought not (let whoever reads this understand), (Matthew 24:15; and Mark 13:14a)

THE ADMONITION: Then let those in Judea flee to the mountains, let those who are in the midst of her depart, and let not those who are in the country enter her. For these are the days of vengeance, that all things which are written may be fulfilled. (Luke 21:21-22)

THE ADMONITION: Then let those in Judea flee to the mountains. Let him who is on the housetop not go down into the house, *nor* enter to take anything out of his house. And let him who is in the field not go back to get his clothes. (Matthew 4:16-18; and Mark 13:b-16)

THE WOE: But woe to those who are pregnant and to those nursing babies in those days_ (Luke 21:23a)

THE WOE: But woe to those who are pregnant and to those with nursing babies in those days. And pray that your flight may not be in the winter or on the Sabbath. (Matthew 24: 19-20; and Mark 13:17-18).

THE EXTENT: For there will be great distress in the land and upon this people. And they will fall by the edge of the sword, and be led away captive into all nations. And Jerusalem will be trampled by Gentiles until the times of the Gentiles are fulfilled. (Luke 21:24)

THE EXTENT: For then, *in* those days, there will be great tribulation such as has not been since the beginning of the creation of the world which God created until this time, no, nor ever shall be. And unless the Lord had shortened those days, no flesh would be saved; but for the elect's sake, whom He chose, He shortened the days (Matthew 24:19-22; and Mark 13:17-20).

As can be seen these two prophesies are parallel in structure. This comparison chart has been divided into four distinct parts of these events: the sign, the admonition, the woe, and the extent of the upcoming devastation. The similarity of these prophesies, however, breaks down at this point, as the contents are compared to one another.

Let us begin by examining the signs. In Luke, the sign is that of an army surrounding Jerusalem. While in Matthew and Mark the sign is the *abomination of desolation*. The question then is, "Do these two signs represent the same event?" Frederick Godet says that they do, indeed, represent the same thing. He states that there is no reason why we should not recognize the Roman standards planted outside the city walls as the abomination standing in the holy place, where it ought not.[1] There are, however, two very good reasons for distinguishing the Roman standards from the *abomination of desolation*. First, the Roman standards had been placed outside of Jerusalem's walls on many occasions, making them unlikely candidates as a sign which would be readily recognized to the people of the city, whereas seeing the army itself actually surround the city would have been something new for the residents of the city to view. Furthermore, such an interpretation stretches the commonly accepted meaning of the expression "the holy place." To the Jewish mind, of the first century at least, the words "the holy place" could only represent the temple itself.[2] An army surrounding the city would not be the same as an abomination standing in the holy place. Moreover, if the *abomination of desolation* were to represent a later planting of Roman standards or statue in the temple courts or even the burning, looting, and dismantling of the temple, then the admonitions to flee in Matthew and Mark would have

---

1   Frederick Godet, <u>A Commentary on the Gospel of St. Luke</u>, trans. by M.D. Cusin (Edinburg: T&T Clark, n.d.), II, 266.

2   Flavius Josephus shows the importance which was given to the temple and its inner court, as being called holy; see Flavius Josephus, <u>The Wars of the Jews</u> in <u>The Works of Flavius Josephus</u>, trans. by William Whiston (New York: A.L. Burt Company, Publishers, n.d.), V, i, 2.

been of little value to the inhabitants of the city. For, from the time that Titus began the siege of the city in A.D. 70 until the end of the war, the inhabitants of Jerusalem were given no opportunity to escape the terrors of the devastating assault.[3]

The admonition of the Luke account is very much like the admonitions of Matthew and Mark. Matthew and Mark are slightly more explicit in their warning, and Luke includes the phrase "For these are the days of vengeance, that all things which are written may be fulfilled …"(Luke 21:22). Other than these differences, the two prophesies' admonitions could be talking about the same event. The question then becomes, "What is meant by 'the days of vengeance?'" The Old Testament prophecies regarding the time of Jacob's trouble seem to be silent with regard to a specific vengeance, though they do speak of a general wrath which will be poured out on the whole world. This phrase, however, appears to be speaking of a specific vengeance.

To understand the question of the days of vengeance, we need to look at one of the events which led up to Jesus' crucifixion (Matthew 27:15-26). Having been tried before Herod and Pilate, neither of whom could find just cause for executing Him, Jesus was led out before the crowds. Pilate, wanting to appease the multitudes, gave them a choice of prisoners who could be released, Jesus or Barabbas, believing that they would choose Jesus. The chief priests and elders, however, had paid the masses to ask for the release of Barabbas and the death of Jesus. Pilate tried to talk them out of their decision. He went so far as to wash his hands before the crowds to show that he would not be responsible

---

3   Even though Titus relaxed his siege at one point for a period of about four days, no one was able to escape the city because of the seditious element within the city. Those who tried to desert to the Romans were often mutilated. For details, see Josephus, V, ix, 1-2; xiii, 4.

for the shedding of innocent blood, after which he turned Jesus over to be crucified. At this point, the crowd responded with the shout, "His blood be on us and on our children" (Matthew 27:25). In so doing the people made themselves responsible for the shedding of Christ's innocent blood. This was something which would bring about vengeance.

Moreover, Jesus, in closing His rebuke of the hypocritical leadership of Jerusalem, said the following:

> Therefore, indeed, I send you prophets, wise men, and scribes: *some* of them you will kill and crucify, and *some* of them you will scourge in your synagogues and persecute from city to city, that on you may come all the righteous blood shed on the earth, from the blood of righteous Abel to the blood of Zechariah, son of Berechiah, whom you murdered between the temple and the altar. Assuredly, I say to you, all these things will come upon this generation. (Matthew 23:33-36)

The book of Acts testifies of men who went before these leaders, and what was done to them. Vengeance belongs to the Lord, and He will repay (Deuteronomy 32:35; and Romans 12:19). The religious leaders of Jerusalem brought the blood of Jesus Christ upon themselves, the people, and the children of the people. Vengeance came upon that generation in the form of the destruction of the city in A.D. 70, and what was written was fulfilled.

The woes pronounced in both of these prophecies are the same, with the exception of the added command to pray that these things wouldn't come in the winter or on the Sabbath, found in Matthew and Mark. Both the fall of Jerusalem and the future demise of the city during the great tribulation was and will be times of great horror. Therefore, there is no surprise that the same words of woe appear in both prophecies. The added emphasis of prayer in Matthew and Mark may suggest an increased intensity of the later devastation, but otherwise these are both depicting the woes of very troublesome times.

Now, when the extent of these devastations is compared, there is a notable contrast. The Luke passage speaks of great distress for the land and the people, whereas, in Matthew and Mark, Jesus declares that there will be a time of tribulation such as has never been before nor will be afterward. Certainly the demise of Jerusalem in A.D. 70 brought about great distress to the land and the people, but one could hardly say that there hasn't been or will ever be an event as devastating as the fall of Jerusalem in A.D. 70. On the other hand, the book of the Revelation describes a devastation which is unparalleled in all of history. At one point, one fourth of the world's population will die (Revelation 6:8). Then not long after that disaster, another one third of the remaining population will die (Revelation 9:18). The language of the prophecy in Matthew and Mark matches that kind of devastation.

Luke 21:23-24 reads as follows:

> And they will fall by the edge of the sword, and be led away captive into all nations. And Jerusalem will be trampled by the Gentiles until the times of the Gentiles are fulfilled. (Luke 21:23-24)

The question which arises out of this segment in "What was Jesus referring to as 'the times of the Gentiles'?" Perhaps the answer is found in the book of Daniel chapter 9. Daniel 9:24-27 presents a prophecy, often referred to as the Seventy Weeks. The prophecy is concerning the people of Israel and the holy city of Jerusalem. In the prophecy there are "seven weeks and sixty-two weeks" or sixty-nine weeks until the cutting off of the Messiah. The weeks here are literally "sevens" or seven year periods of time. Then a gap appears before the prince who is to come confirms a covenant with many for one week or seven years. The gap is what we would like to examine. The content of the gap is as follows:

> ... And the people of the prince who is to come shall destroy the city and the sanctuary. The end of it shall be with a flood, and till the end of the war desolations are determined. (Daniel 9:26b)

That gap represents a period of Gentile domination over the people of Israel and the city of Jerusalem. Hence the gap between the sixty-ninth week and the seventieth week of Daniel 9 is "the times of the Gentiles." During that time, the people of the prince who is to come (i.e., the Romans) destroy the city and the sanctuary (i.e., Titus' siege of Jerusalem in A.D. 70). And desolations (plural) are determined, which is represented by the Gentiles trampling Jerusalem under foot.

The destruction of Jerusalem, as well as the dismantling of the temple, are historical facts. Jesus warned the disciples and those who followed them to steer clear of Jerusalem when the armies began their march on the city. This warning may have saved the lives of many Christians during that horrible war. Henry Alford comments that there is no record of any Christians who perished in the siege of Jerusalem.[4] Moreover, we can note that Jerusalem has been trodden by the Gentiles ever since its destruction.

Looking back over the previous chapters of the discourse, we see that Jesus began by warning His disciples against false messiahs. He told them not to be troubled by wars and natural disasters. These things, He said, would come

---

4   Henry Alford, <u>The Greek Testament</u>, revised by Everett F. Harrison (Chicago: Moody Press, 1958), I, 238.

of necessity, but were not necessarily the signs which would indicate the end of the age or His return. There were matters of greater concern for the disciples to consider: matters of persecution and trials, and even their own deaths. Most importantly, however, the message of the gospel would continue to be preached throughout the world.

As many Christians today, we may not face the persecutions and trials that the apostles faced (though there are those that do), and though there may come a time when we will. Yet the principles which Jesus showed to His disciples are still the same. We can get caught up with looking at the disturbances in our world taking place around us and conclude that the end is coming, and begin to chase after what may appear to be indications of His return, or we can realize that these things must come to pass, and concentrate on the calling which Christ has given us. We need also to realize that the calling that we have received may lead to persecutions and trials, and we need to understand that it is not in our own abilities and strengths that we should confide, but rather our confidence and strength comes from Jesus, and the power of the Holy Spirit Who dwells within us and directs us.

CHAPTER 7
GENERAL WARNINGS TO THE MANY

At this point in the discourse, a change in focus takes place. Whereas the previous chapters dealt with issues directly related to the disciples and the inhabitants of Jerusalem during the first century A.D., this passage is directed toward the "many." This is what Jesus had to say about the "many":

> And then many will be offended, will betray one another, and will hate one another. Then many false prophets will rise up and deceive many. And because lawlessness will abound, the love of many will grow cold. But he who endures to the end shall be saved. And this gospel of the kingdom will be preached in the world as a witness to all the nations, and then the end will come. (Matthew 24:10-14, Mark 13:13b)

Jesus begins these verses with the words, "And then many..." The first question that comes to mind is "When is then?"

These verses appear to be a transition between the answers to the disciples' questions, "Teacher, tell us when will these things be? And what sign will there be when these things are about to take place?" (Luke 21:7) and "And what *will be* the sign of Your coming, and the end of the age, when all these things will be fulfilled?" (Matthew 24:3, Mark 13:4). The word "then," therefore, would seem to be a reference to Daniel's seventieth week or the great tribulation. There are other indicators within these verses which would seem to verify this conclusion.

Jesus points out that, during this period of time, "… many will be offended, will betray one another, and will hate one another" (Matthew 24:10). This is the antithesis to what it means to be a disciple of Jesus. They will be offended. The question would be, "offended at what or who?" The answer would seem to be at Jesus and His message of the Kingdom. The word "offended" is translated from the Greek word *skandalizo,* from which we get the English word "scandalize."[1] These people will be scandalized at Jesus. Jesus said, earlier in Matthew, "… And blessed is he who is not offended because of Me" (Matthew 11:6). The same word *skandalizo* is used here. The offence will go so far as to result in betrayal and hatred of one another. These attributes will characterize many during the tribulation period.

Also, during that time, many false prophets will rise up, resulting in the deception of many (Matthew 24:11). There were false prophets before the first coming of Christ, and there have been and are false teachers presently, who have led and currently lead many astray (II Peter 2:1-2). Jesus says, here, that false prophets will again deceive many during the tribulation. The apostle Paul wrote,

---

1   <u>Strong's Exhaustive Concordance of the Bible,</u> <u>The Old Time Gospel</u> <u>Hour Edition</u> (Lynchburg, Virginia; Dr. Jerry Falwell, director, n.d.), Greek Dictionary of the New Testament p.65, ref. 4624

"And for this reason God will send them strong delusion, that they should believe the lie, that they all may be condemned who did not believe the truth but had pleasure in unrighteousness" (II Thessalonians 2:11-12).

Another indicator that this portion of the discourse is directed toward the tribulation period is that "... lawlessness will abound, ..." (Matthew 24:12). In writing to the Thessalonians, Paul stated,

"For the mystery of lawlessness is already at work; only, He who now restrains *will do so* until He is taken out of the way. And then the lawless one will be revealed, whom the Lord will consume with the breath of His mouth and destroy with the brightness of His coming" (II Thessalonians 2:7-8).

The principle of lawlessness is already at work in the world, but it is currently being restrained. There is coming a time when the Restrainer (the Holy Spirit) will no longer restrain, and lawlessness will abound.

The result of this lawlessness is that, "... the love of many will grow cold" (Matthew 24:12) The Greek word for "love" here is *agapao* meaning: to love, value, esteem, feel or manifest generous concern for, be faithful towards; to delight in; to set store upon.[2] The love in view here is a faithfulness toward God manifesting a generous concern for others. Perhaps the fear of betrayal or reprisal will cause many to grow cold in their love. Nonetheless these will be treacherous days in which many saints of God will die (see Revelation 7:9-17). People from all over the world will be martyred for their testimony of Jesus and His Kingdom.

---

2   The Analytical Greek Lexicon Revised, edited by Harold K. Moulton (Grand Rapids, Michigan: Zondervan Publishing House, 1977), p. 2.

Jesus went on to say, "But he who endures to the end shall be saved" (Matthew 24:13; Mark 13:13) The word "But" shows that this is being contrasted against that which came before. In spite of the tremendous peril of the great tribulation, some will endure to the end. The word "endure" carries the idea of holding up under some kind of pressure. In this case those who endure are those who remain faithful toward God under the pressure of betrayal, hatred, and the very real threat of death.

The "end" is a word which could have many meanings. Technically the end means a terminal or stopping point. In this case, that terminal point seems to be the close of the tribulation period. John Walvoord, therefore, suggests that the phrase "… he who endure to the end …" is in reference to those who endure through the tribulation period.[3] Another suggestion, relating to individuals is that the end is a reference to death. Jesus used this expression, "But he who endures to the end shall be saved" (Matthew 10:22), in an earlier point of His ministry, when commissioning the twelve. In that case, physical death seems to be a plausible definition, since He was addressing the twelve directly. Remember, one of the twelve did not endure to the end, namely Judas Iscariot. He ended his own life after betraying the Lord Jesus Christ (John 18:2, Acts 1:18-19). In this case, however, the people whom Jesus appears to be referencing are those who will have endured the great tribulation and will be still alive. Also "the end" in this phrase is in close proximity to the phrase, "and then the end shall come," (Matthew 24:14) which might suggest that they are a reference to the same time. The later reference to the end seems clearly to be a reference to the end of the age, which would coincide with the end of the great tribulation, making John Walvoord's

---

3   John F. Walvoord, <u>Matthew: Thy Kingdom Come</u> (Chicago: Moody Press, 1974), p. 184.

suggestion the most plausible conclusion for the meaning of the end in this phrase. Perhaps both meanings could apply for this phrase: physical death for those martyred during the tribulation, and the end of the age for those who survive that time.

The obvious meaning of the words "shall be saved" would be spiritual salvation. However, the Greek word *sothesetai* meaning "shall be saved" does not always mean spiritual salvation. This word comes from the root verb *sozo* which has a variety of meanings, including: to save, to rescue, and to preserve safe and unharmed.[4] The question here is, "Do any of these meanings fit more appropriately than spiritual salvation?" Since this phrase is parallel to one quoted in connection with Jesus' disciples, in which Jesus was obviously talking about spiritual salvation, the most appropriate fit here is that of spiritual salvation. Moreover, in Daniel 12:12, those who wait to the end of the age are called "blessed," which is a word reserved for the spiritually saved.

The final verse in this portion of the discourse is good news indeed. It says, "And this gospel of the kingdom will be preached in all the world as a witness to all nations, and then the end will come" (Matthew 24:14). E. Schuyler English attributes the entire first part of the Olivet Discourse to the tribulation period on the basis of the use of the term "gospel of the kingdom," which he believes belongs strictly to "the Jewish age." In doing so, he makes a sharp distinction between "the gospel of the kingdom" and "the gospel of grace."[5] This writer views such a distinction as a false one. The preaching of the good news regarding the Kingdom of God did not cease with the advent of the age of grace. The

---

4 <u>The Analytical Greek Lexicon Revised</u>, p. 395.
5 E. Schuyler English, <u>Studies in the Gospel According to Matthew</u> (New York: Our Hope Publication, 1925), pp 170-173.

apostle Peter implicitly preached the offer of the kingdom in his sermon on the day of Pentecost (Acts 2:14-36) As the Church spread into Samaria, Philip preached both "the things concerning the kingdom of God and the name of Jesus Christ" (Acts 8:12). As Paul and Barnabas made the return portion of their first missionary endeavor, they encouraged those who accepted Christ, and exhorted them by saying, "We must through many tribulations enter the kingdom of God" (Acts 14:22). As Paul witnessed in the synagogue at Ephesus, he reasoned and persuaded for three months "concerning the things of the kingdom of God" (Acts 19:8). In Paul's parting words at Ephesus, as he headed for Jerusalem, Paul stated,

> But none of these things move me; nor do I count my life dear to myself, so that I may finish my race with joy, and the ministry which I received from the Lord Jesus, <u>to testify to the gospel of the grace of God</u>. And indeed, now I know that you all, among whom <u>I have gone preaching the kingdom of God</u>, will see my face no more [underlining this writer's] (Acts 20:24-25)

As the book of Acts closes, Paul was still found preaching the kingdom of God (Acts 28: 23, 31). In his epistles, Paul emphasized the kingdom (Romans 14:17; I Corinthians 4:20, 6:9-10, 15:50; Galatians 5:21; Ephesians 5:5; Colossians 1:13, 4:11; I Thessalonians 2:12; II Thessalonians 1:5; II Timothy 4: 1, 18). For Paul, the preaching of the grace of Christ and the preaching of His kingdom were integrally related. Jesus offered the keys of the kingdom to His disciples (Matthew 16:19). Those keys consist of the grace of God, which He displayed in the giving of His only Son to be a substitutionary sacrifice for the sins of the world, "that whoever believes in Him should not perish but have everlasting life" (John 3:16;

I Corinthians 15:1-4; Matthew 16:21). The kingdom of God and the grace of God are integral parts of the same gospel. Both deserve preaching in our world today.

Many missionary ventures today have taken on the task of reaching every people group (*ethnos*) with the gospel of Jesus Christ. Whether they will reach their goal before Daniel's seventieth week arrives is yet to be seen. But Jesus has assured us that "this gospel of the kingdom will be preached in all the world as a witness to all the nations" (Matthew 24:14). The testimony of Revelation 7 shows that the preaching of the gospel will continue during the tribulation period.

As for the principle of lawlessness mentioned in this portion of the discourse, it has been at work since the beginning of the Church age, and is becoming ever more prevalent. There is coming a time when the Restrainer will no longer restrain and the lawless one will work his wonders and signs of deception. The need for us as Christians today is to endure, or "stand fast" as the apostle Paul has stated it (I Corinthians 16:13; Galatians 5:1). The end will come at the appointed time, but in the interim we have a calling to stand fast in the strength of the Lord.

Chapter 8
The Abomination of Desolation

According to chapters three through five, Jesus opened the Olivet Discourse by dispelling the notion that the end of the age and His second coming would come immediately. He specifically warned the disciples against coming rumors which might indicate His return. He also taught the disciples with regard to the things which they would suffer for the sake of the spread of the gospel of the Kingdom. Through all of this, Jesus stressed that the "end" was not yet.

In chapter six, we saw that Luke recorded the sign which would announce the desolation of Jerusalem and the destruction of the temple. Here, we also saw that Jesus was separating the disciples' questions. The disciples had lumped all of their questions together, as if all of the events were to happen simultaneously. Jesus in His reply, however, separated the answer concerning Jerusalem's desolation and the destruction of the temple from the answer to the remaining question: "And what *will be* the sign of your coming, and the end of the age, when all these things will be fulfilled?" (Matthew 24:3, Mark 13:4). In a sense the disciples were correct in thinking that the end of the age and

Jesus' return would be the fulfillment of all these things, but they lacked the comprehension to realize that there would be an interlude between the time of Jerusalem's desolation and the return of Jesus.

Having shown the disciples that the end would not come immediately and that Jerusalem's desolation would not be the sign that the end was coming soon, Jesus began to teach the disciples with regard to those things which would mark the end as being very near. In chapter seven, Jesus transitioned from the "times of the Gentiles" to "Daniel's seventieth week." In that chapter, we saw the conditions which would make things very difficult for the "many" that would remain faithful to God during the great tribulation.

At this point in the discourse, Jesus discloses the signal which will mark the end of the age and His soon return. The following is the record of that sign:

> Therefore when you see the *"abomination of desolation*," spoken of by Daniel the prophet, standing in the holy place, where it ought not (let whoever reads understand), then let those who are in Judea flee to the mountains. Let him who is on the housetop not go down into the house, [nor] enter to take anything out of his house. And let him who is in the field not go back to get his clothes. But woe to those who are pregnant and those who are nursing babies in those days. And pray that your flight may not be in winter or on the Sabbath. For then, *in* those days, there will be great tribulation such as has not been since the beginning of the creation of the world, which God created, until this time, no, nor ever shall be. And unless the Lord had shortened those days no flesh would be saved; but

> for the elect's sake, whom He chose, He shortened
> the days. (Matthew 24: 15-22, Mark 13: 14-20)

The words "when you see" give this warning the appearance of being addressed to Jesus' disciples. However, there is an additional phrase in the opening sentence of this paragraph which redefines the audience as "whoever reads" (Matthew 24:15) or "the reader" (Mark 13:14). This phrase has been placed in parentheses, (let whoever reads this understand), to indicate that these words were something which the writers of the gospels had interjected, rather than being words which Jesus had actually spoken. They do, however, identify the audience as those who would read this prophecy at some unspecified future date. Though these words are parenthetical to the words which Jesus spoke in the discourse, they are nonetheless words which were inspired by the Holy Spirit, and are, therefore, to be understood as being significant to the text.

Perhaps the two audiences, the apostles themselves and whoever reads can be explained in the following manner. The apostles may well be witnesses of the events herein described, but not in their physical bodies. The writer of the book of Hebrews, after having delineated a list of men and women of faith, turned to his readers and stated, "Therefore we also, since we are surrounded by so great a cloud of witnesses, …" (Hebrews 12:1). Many conservative commentators believe that these men and women of faith are, in fact, witnessing, from heaven, the events which are occurring even now. That being the case, we can conclude that the apostles, who were also great men of faith, will be witnesses of the events which will take place in the future. Moreover, since the apostles and other saints [believers in Jesus Christ] of this age have already passed into the presence of the Lord (Philippians 1:23), those who will need to heed these admonitions are those who will physically witness the unfolding of this prophecy. By addressing the disciples in this manner, Jesus was able to maintain a sense of immanency with regard to His return and the establishment of the Kingdom. This is something which Jesus continued to do on the day of His ascension into heaven (Acts 16:7). So, we can see that there are, in fact, two sets of witnesses to the unveiling of this prophecy, those who will be physically present and those who will have gone on before to be present with the Lord.

Before getting into the details of this prophecy, this is just a reminder that this prophecy is separate from the prophecy found in Luke 21. In chapter six of this book, this writer compared these two prophecies and concluded that the prophecy in Luke 21 concerned the period surrounding the destruction of Jerusalem in A.D. 70. This prophecy, on the other hand, is connected to the time known as the great tribulation, as described in the book of the Revelation.

Let us begin our examination of this prophecy by looking at the phrase. "the *'abomination of desolation,'* spoken of by Daniel the prophet ..." (Matthew 24:15 and Mark 13:14). The prophet Daniel made but three references to abominations in his book (Daniel 9:27, 11:31, and 12:11). According to John Walvoord, the prophecy of Daniel 11:31 had its fulfillment under the reign of Antiochus Epiphanes who ruled Syria from 176 to 165 B.C., while the other two prophecies are in reference to the same future event which will take place during the time of the great tribulation.[1] This writer concurs with Walvoord's findings.

Obviously, as Jesus spoke to His disciples on the slope of Olivet, He was not referring, in any direct sense, to the desecration of the temple which took place during the reign of Antiochus Epiphanes. That abomination took place

---

1   John F. Walvoord, "Christ's Olivet Discourse on the End of the Age," <u>Bibliotheca Sacra</u>, 128 (October, 1971): 318-320.

before the first advent of Christ, and Jesus was talking about something which was yet to happen. However, the abomination of the temple under the reign of Antiochus can serve as a type of that which is to come, and depending on how closely the two events parallel one another, that incident may shed some light on the nature of the event which will occur during the latter days.

When Antiochus took Jerusalem, he spoiled the temple, caused the daily sacrifice to cease, dissolved the Jewish laws, prevented circumcision, offered swine's flesh on the altar, and allowed the most extreme cruelty to be performed on the inhabitants.[2] Besides these blasphemous acts, he ordered the erection of "a desolating sacrilege [probably a statue of the Greek god, Zeus] upon the altar of offering."[3] This statue represented the abomination of desolation spoken by Daniel the prophet (Daniel 11:31). If this description of the abomination of desolation is indeed a foreshadowing of the future event, then the event in Luke 21 in no way matches this. However, according to Paul's second letter to the Thessalonians, when the "lawless one," "the man of sin" is revealed, he will exalt himself as God, in the temple of God (II Thessalonians 2:3, 4, and 8), and this would parallel Antiochus' abomination of desolation. Antiochus set up a desolating sacrilege upon the altar of offering within the temple, the man of sin will set himself up as God himself within the temple. This latter act of blasphemy will amount to the ultimate sacrilege.

---

2 Flavius Josephus, The wars of the Jews in The Works of Flavius Josephus, trans. by William Whiston (New York: A.L. Burt Company, Publishers, n.d.), I, i, 1-2.

3 Bruce Metzger, ed., The Apocrypha of the Old Testament: Revised Standard Version (New York: Oxford University Press, 1973), I Maccabees 1:54, II Maccabees 6:2.

Daniel 9:27 and 12:11 both describe yet future events which are set to occur approximately three and a half years before the conclusion of the time set aside for the completion of the restoration of the nation of Israel. Daniel 9 presents a prophecy known as the "seventy weeks." According to Daniel 9:27, the prince who is to come will make a pact with Israel for one week (seven years), and, in the midst of that week, he commits abominations. Daniel 12 identifies this time as the "time of trouble" on the nation (Daniel 12:1). The prophet Jeremiah refers to this time as "Jacob's trouble" (Jeremiah 30:7). Both Daniel 9:27 and Daniel 12:11 call for the taking away of the daily sacrifice and the abomination of desolation to happen somewhere around three and a half years prior to the completion of Israel's restoration. Thus, we see that this sign does, in fact, give a close approximation to the time when the end of the age will occur.

As a matter of record, there are a few conservative scholars who have attributed these prophesies to neither the fall of Jerusalem in A.D. 70 nor to the period of the great tribulation. Both Henry Alford and R.C.H. Lenski place the fulfillment of these prophesies to an uprising which occurred sometime prior to the fall of Jerusalem.[4] At a time before the Roman armies arrived to surround Jerusalem, a band of Jewish zealots secured the inner court of the temple. These zealots sent to the Idumeans claiming that Ananus had betrayed the city. Nearly 200,000 Idumeans came out and surrounded the city, but were not able to enter because the gates were barred shut. During a stormy night the zealots devised a plot to cut the bars of the gates, allowing access to the Idumeans, who then stormed the

---

4   Henry Alford, <u>Alford's Greek Testament</u> (Grand Rapids, Michigan: Guardian Press, 1976), I, 239; and R.C.H. Lenski, <u>The Interpretation of St. Matthews Gospel</u> (Minneapolis, Minnesota: Augsburg Publishing House, 1961), p. 938.

city and joined forces with the zealots and overpowered the guards. These two bloodthirsty groups then took over the city killing the guards, the priests, and the most prominent citizens. According to Josephus, 8,500 men were slaughtered in a single day.[5] Alford and Lenski call this event the "abomination of desolation," because the inner court had been polluted with the blood of innocent men.[6] Again this account falls short of the kind of abomination which took place under Antiochus, and would therefore seem to fall short of the abomination of desolation spoken of by Daniel the prophet. Moreover, this interpretation has considerable difficulty in accounting for the extent of the devastation as described in the Matthew and Mark prophecies.

Both the Luke 21 prophecy and this prophecy give stern admonitions to flee Judea. This is in anticipation of the horrific events which will follow. In Luke, there is the addition of a phrase indicating that the events are attached to specific judgment on the hypocritical leadership of Jerusalem. In this prophecy, however, there is no such indictment indicated.

The admonition to flee is followed by a woe to pregnant women and nursing mothers. No doubt this woe is due to tremendous hardships which will follow. This prophecy also includes the sentence, "And pray that your flight may not be in winter or on the Sabbath" (Matthew 24:20, Mark 13:18). Apparently these times would impede their flight to the mountains or make the hardships of the journey even more difficult.

The extent of the devastation described in this prophecy is so catastrophic that it is really beyond comprehension. The magnitude of this tribulation is such that if it were not cut short, no one would survive (Matthew 24:20). This is

---

5   Josephus, IV, iv; v, 1.
6   Alford, p. 239; Lenski, p. 938.

obviously a time which no one would relish living through. But, praise God, there will be a remnant, whom He has chosen, that will survive.

As a premillenial pretribulational dispensationalist, this writer does not believe that those belonging to the Church will go through this tribulation. This passage, however, should impact our age, insomuch as we have the opportunity to reach the lost with the gospel of the Kingdom, before they are faced with these terrible events. This should be motivation to us to be about the work of evangelizing the world we live in. This writer is convinced that the coming of Daniel's seventieth week is not far in the future. We, as Christians, have a responsibility for spreading the gospel while we can.

CHAPTER 9
THE SECOND WARNING OF DECEPTION

Jesus opened this discourse by warning His disciples against deception, telling them that there would be false christs that they were not to go after. At this point in the discourse Jesus repeats the warning against false christs. Only this time it is not directed at the disciples, but at those who will be looking for the Messiah during the tribulation period. This is what Jesus says to those who will be looking for His appearance:

> Then if anyone says to you, "Look, here *is* the Christ_" or "Look, *He is* there_" do not believe *it*. For false christs and false prophets will arise and show signs and wonders, so as to deceive, if possible, even the elect. But take heed; see, I have told you all things beforehand. Therefore if they say to you, "Look, He is in the desert!" do not go out; or "Look, *He is* in the inner rooms_" do not believe *it*. For as lighting comes from the east and flashes in the west, so also will the coming of the Son of Man be. For wherever the carcass is, there the eagles will be

gathered together. (Matthew 24: 23-28, Mark 13: 21-23)

By this time the lawless one will have been revealed, and those that understand the meaning of that revelation, will also understand that the return of Christ will follow in short order. Jesus is emphatic about not being deceived by false reports of His appearing. Deception will be widespread during this time, and many will willingly follow after the rumors of Christ's return.

Paul, the apostle, told the Thessalonian believers that when the lawless one is revealed his actions would be as follows:

> The coming of the *lawless one* is according to the working of Satan, with all power, signs and lying wonders, and with all unrighteous deception among those who perish, because they did not receive the love of the truth, that they might be saved. (II Thessalonians 2:9, 10)

Jesus' warning is to the elect [those who believe in Him], and He warns that the false prophets and false christs would deceive even the elect, if possible. Paul, in speaking to the Thessalonians, goes on to say about those who perish that, "...God will send them strong delusion, that they should believe the lie, that they all may be condemned who did not believe the truth but had pleasure in unrighteousness." (II Thessalonians 2:11, 12) With regard to the rumors Jesus says "do not go out" and "do not believe it." Jesus tells the elect that His coming will be clearly visible, like the flashing of lightening.

Jesus states, "For wherever the carcass is, there the eagles will be gathered together." (Matthew 24:28) The carcass here represents the dead. When Jesus returns, there will terrible carnage. Unbelievers during the tribulation are as good as dead. The eagles are vultures seeking to feed on the dead bodies. Thus, the vultures seek to feed on those who are lost. Perhaps the vultures represent the false prophets and false christs who desire to lead unbelievers after themselves. Jesus' warning to believers is clear, they are to steer away from the rumors of His return.

These warnings are given specifically for those who will be present during the last three and a half years of the great tribulation, but can also serve the Church well today. There are a multitude of false teachings concerning Jesus Christ being spread in our present world by the antichrists of our day (I John 2:18-25). These false teachings are deceptions designed to draw people away from the Truth. Jesus said, "I am the way, the truth, and the life. No one comes to the Father except through Me" (John14:6). Many today are tempted to follow strange doctrines for whatever reason. Yet, there is only one true way, and that is the way that Jesus leads, through His Word. The warning, though intended for the tribulation saints, issues forth sound advice, "Don't believe the rumors." The apostle Peter put it this way, "Be sober, be vigilant; because your adversary the devil walks about like a roaring lion, seeking whom he may devour." (I Peter 5:8) If we "… grow in the grace and knowledge of our Lord and Savior Jesus Christ," then we will not be, "… led away with the error of the wicked" (II Peter 3:17-18).

Chapter 10
Signs in Heaven and on Earth

At the outset of this discourse Jesus told His disciples to beware of imposters, after which He explained that there would be wars and rumors of wars, natural disasters, and heavenly disturbances. He pointed out that these would not be the signs of the end of the age, but that they must come to pass first. In doing so, Jesus indicated that, as the time for the end approached, such activities would continue like birth pains prior to delivery. Now, at this point in the discourse, Jesus shows the extent to which natural disasters and heavenly disturbances will reach as the end of the age actually approaches. The following are the words Jesus used to describe the conditions that will be evident on the face of the earth at the end of this corrupt age:

> But in those days, immediately after that tribulation, there will be signs in the sun, in the moon, and in the stars; the sun will be darkened, and the moon will not give its light; the stars will fall from heaven. And on the earth there will be distress of nations, with perplexity, the sea and the waves roaring; men's

hearts failing them for fear and the expectation of
those things which are coming on the earth, for the
powers of the heavens will be shaken. (Matthew
24:29, Mark 13:24-25, Luke 21:25-26)

There is a view of this discourse, which attempts to place
the entire discourse in the past, which has its fulfillment
coinciding with the destruction of Jerusalem in A.D. 70.
This is sometimes referred to as the historical fulfillment
view.[1] Proponents of this view, however, in placing the above
conditions to the time surrounding the fall of Jerusalem,
admit that these words cannot be taken literally, and still
be referring to the fall of Jerusalem in A.D. 70. These
commentators must resort to an allegorical method of
interpretation in order to make these words fit the era which
they believe it should fit. For example, J. Marcellus Kik
writes the following with regard to Matthew 24:29:

If the sun, moon, and stars refer to the Jewish
nation and its prerogatives, then we have seen the
fulfillment of this prophecy. The Jewish nation has
been darkened and no longer shines for God. This
has been true ever since the tribulation of those
days. God in His righteous wrath has removed the
Jewish nation from His heavens. The sun of Judaism
has been darkened, as the moon it no longer reflects
the Light of God, bright stars as were the prophets
no longer shine in the Israel of the flesh.[2]

---

1   J. Marcellus Kik, Matthew Twenty-four: An Exposition (Swengal,
    Pennsylvania: Bible Truth Depot, n.d.), p. 65; Loraine Boettner, The
    Millennium (Grand Rapids, Michigan: Baker Book House, 1958), pp.
    254-8; and Frederick Godet, A Commentary on the Gospel of St. Luke,
    trans. by M.D. Cusin (Edinburg: T&T Clark, n.d.), II, pp. 268-70.
2   Kik, p.65.

Loraine Boettner calls this portion "pictorial language."[3] Frederick Godet follows the same reasoning when commenting on Luke 21:25.[4] Such reasoning assumes that these words cannot be understood literally, since heavenly disturbances of this nature have never been seen before. Such assumptions are not necessary. There have been many prophecies of the Old Testament which had not been seen before they were literally fulfilled in Jesus Christ's first advent. Therefore, there is no reason to assume that, because something has not occurred in the past, it cannot occur in the future. In fact, in speaking of the devastation associated with the *abomination of desolation*, Jesus said: "For then, in those days, there will great tribulation such as has not been since the beginning of the creation of the world, which God created, until this time, no nor ever shall be." (Matthew 24:21; Mark 13:19).

Jesus had been speaking to His disciples in a literal fashion up to this juncture of the discourse, and there is no reason found in the words that He spoke or otherwise to assume that He had changed to using figurative speech. A text can made to fit most anything that a person has preconceived, by discarding its literal meaning for figurative language. All that is needed is to assign the appropriate figures to the words. Certainly, the Bible does employ figurative language, but when it does there are appropriate indications that a figure is about to be used.

These words speak of a time, "immediately after that tribulation" (Matthew 24:29; Mark 13:24). Jesus was referring to the tribulation that would follow the *abomination of desolation*. When the Antichrist exalts himself as God within the temple, he will also turn against the nation of Israel and the city of Jerusalem. At that time, horrible

3   Boettner, p. 255.
4   Godet, pp. 269-270.

tribulation will come on the people of Israel. The prophet Zechariah describes this kind of tribulation in connection with the coming "day of the LORD." (Zechariah 14:1) Zechariah prophesied:

> Behold, the day of the LORD is
>   coming,
> And your spoil will be divided in
>   your midst.
> For I will gather all the nations to
>   battle against Jerusalem;
> The city shall be taken,
> The houses rifled,
> And the women ravished.
> Half of the city shall go into
>   captivity,
> But the remnant of the people shall
>   not be cut off from the city.
>
> Then the LORD will go forth
> And fight against the nations,
> As He fights in the day of battle.
> And in that day His feet will stand
>   on the Mount of Olives,
> Which faces Jerusalem on the east.
>   (Zechariah 14:1-4a)

As can be seen, Zechariah predicts a time of tribulation for the people of Jerusalem, followed by the return of the LORD. This scene depicted in the Olivet Discourse is a picture of what will take place upon the earth at the time that the LORD comes back to fight against all the nations of the earth.

The book of the Revelation graphically depicts the kinds of things which the Lord has briefly described in this

passage of the discourse. The prophet Joel also wrote the
following:

> Multitudes, multitudes in the valley
>   of decision_
> For the day of the LORD is near in
>   the valley of decision.
> The sun and moon will grow dark
> And the stars will diminish their
>   brightness.
> The LORD also will roar from Zion,
> And utter His voice from Jerusalem;
> The heavens and earth will shake;
> But the LORD will be a shelter for His
>   people,
> And the strength of the children of
>   Israel.
> (Joel 3:14-16)

Moreover, the LORD spoke through the prophet Haggai
saying,

> "For thus says the LORD of hosts: 'Once more (it is
> a little while) I will shake heaven and earth, the sea
> and dry land; and I will shake all nations and they
> shall come to the Desire of All Nations, and I will
> fill this temple with glory,' says the LORD of hosts.
> …" (Haggai 2:6,7)

The LORD will shake heaven and earth before His return,
and the hearts of many will fail, for, though they should
recognize what is coming, they will have been deceived,
because they will have refused to believe the Truth (II
Thessalonians 2:11,12). The LORD will come. His glory will

be seen in all of the earth, and He will fight against all that exalts itself against God, and He shall be Victorious.

This passage and the three passages before it are directed primarily to those who will experience the latter days of the great tribulation. Yet, in a sense, they were spoken for the benefit of all who have accepted Jesus Christ as their LORD and Savior. The warnings are clearly intended to direct those who will experience the trials described in this passage. Yet, Jesus also wanted His disciples and us to understand that the days which are coming are terrible days. They are days which none of us would relish living through. Therefore, they stand as a motivation for us to be about the calling to which God has called us. There are people all around us who are dying in their sins and we have the message of hope. We have received Christ and have a part in His eternal Kingdom, but the world is being deceived and will be deceived by Satan. We know the Truth, and we have a responsibility to make the Truth known. Those who will be deceived in the latter days will be deceived, because they have refused the love of the truth (II Thessalonians 2:11). The return of Christ for His Church is very near. Exactly how near is something which is placed in the Father's authority (Acts 1:7). Maranatha_

CHAPTER 11
THE SIGN OF THE SON OF MAN

In the previous chapter, Jesus showed His disciples that certain heavenly and earthly disturbances will point to His soon return. In chapter nine, Jesus told those who will be present at the time of His return that they will need to avoid rumors of His presence. Moreover, He explained that the sign of His coming would be open and visible. In this chapter, Jesus teaches on the sign of His coming:

> Then the sign of the Son of Man will appear in heaven, and then all the tribes of the earth will mourn, and they will see the Son of Man coming on the clouds of heaven with power and great glory. Now when these things begin to happen, look up and lift up your heads, because your redemption draws near. And He will send His angels with a great sound of a trumpet, and they will gather together His elect from the four winds, from the farthest part of earth to the farthest part of heaven. (Matthew 24: 30-31, Mark 13:26-27, Luke 21: 27-28)

The sign of the Son of Man is clearly an answer to the disciples' question, "And what will be the sign of your coming...?" Jesus' disciples knew that He was going away, though they did not yet understand where that would be. Their concern wasn't with where He was going, at this point, but with when and how He would return. The disciples coupled Christ's return with the end of the age. Jesus seems to indicate, as well, that His return will coincide with the end of the age. Nonetheless, some commentators have attempted to fit this prophecy into the past. Loraine Boettner, for instance, states that the sign of the Son of Man was the manifestation of the Holy Spirit which occurred on the day of Pentecost. He, then, applies the later half of that sentence to the destruction of Jerusalem in A.D. 70. Moreover, the gathering of the elect, in the last sentence of this passage, is interpreted by Boettner as an allusion to the evangelization of the world which began with Peter's sermon on the day of Pentecost and continues throughout the age.[1]

Once again, this type of reasoning ignores the literal meaning of the text, and assigns the interpretation of the passage to the allegorical method. Frederick Godet follows this line of reasoning, as well, in the interpretation of Luke 21:27-28.[2] By following this line of thought, these commentators are forced to do a bit of juggling with the chronological order of the text. These authors place the opening of the first sentence of this passage on the day of Pentecost, and they assign the latter half of the same sentence to the destruction of Jerusalem, nearly thirty-seven years latter. Then they return to the day of Pentecost and Peter's sermon to place the second and third sentences. Not only

---

1   Loraine Boettner, The Millenium (Grand Rapids, Michigan: Baker Book House, 1958), pp. 255-258.

2   Frederick Godet, Commentary on the Gospel of St. Luke, trans by M.D. Cusin (Edinburg: T&T Clark, n.d.), pp.269-271.

do they juggle the timing, but the language of the opening sentence requires a great deal of latitude in order to fit what happened on the day of Pentecost with this description of the sign of the Son of Man.

Undoubtedly the manifestation of the Holy Spirit on the day of Pentecost was a sign sent by the Son of Man, but was it really a sign which appeared in heaven? The passage states that "... the sign of the Son of Man will appear in heaven, ...and they will see the Son of Man coming on the clouds of heaven with power and great glory." (Matthew 24: 30; Mark 13:26; Luke 21:27) According to Acts 2:2-3, there was a sound which came from heaven, but the manifestation of the Holy Spirit appeared only unto those in the house. Again, Jesus said in this passage, "... and then all the tribes of the earth will morns, ..." (Matthew 24:30). While it is true that there were "devout men from every nation under heaven" (Acts 2:5) in Jerusalem on that day, the response of the crowds could hardly be construed as mournful. The masses were said to be confused (Acts 2:6), amazed (Acts 2:7, 12), and even perplexed (Acts 2:41), but no mention is made to their being mournful. The fact is that there was probably a great deal of rejoicing taking place in Jerusalem on the day of Pentecost, as about three thousand souls were added to the Church that day (Acts 2:41). These commentators, then, needed to place the mourning of the tribes to a latter time, namely the destruction of Jerusalem, which doesn't seem to fit any better. Contrariwise, what is described in the Revelation chapter nineteen will give good cause for mourning among all the tribes of the earth.

In addition to the problems stated above, the historical fulfillment view interpretation of this passage is inconsistent with the wording of the text itself. The wording of this sentence connects the sign of the Son of Man with the events of the previous sentence, which reads "in those days, immediately after that tribulation" (Matthew 24:29; Mark 13:24-25). The Greek word *tote* which is translated "then" in the passage (Matthew 24:30; Mark 13:26; Luke 21:27) denotes concurrent or consequent events.[3] Boettner and Godet, however, are in agreement that the tribulation spoken of in the previous text should be assigned to the destruction of Jerusalem in A.D. 70.[4] They end up placing nearly thirty-seven years between this passage and the previous text. Their interpretation forces them to do this, since there is nothing recorded in history surrounding the siege of Jerusalem by Titus which resembles the sign of the Son of Man.

Furthermore, in allegorizing the visible appearance of Jesus into a spiritual presence of the Lord's judgment, Boettner and Godet seem to ignore the fact that the disciples had specifically asked Jesus about His return at the end of the age.[5] There is no indication within this text to suggest that this should be understood as anything other than the Lord's visible return to the earth at the end of the age. The men in white who stood by on Olivet, while Jesus ascended into heaven, said to His disciples, "Men of Galilee why do you stand gazing into heaven? This same Jesus, who was taken up from you into heaven, will so come in like manner as you saw Him go into heaven" (Acts 1:11). Jesus ascended into heaven visibly and He will return visibly. The prophet Zechariah connects this visible return of Jesus with the day of the LORD, which takes place at the close of the Jewish age (Zechariah 14:1-4). The disciples wanted to know about Jesus' return at the end of the age, and this passage is Jesus' answer to that question.

---

3   W.E. Vine, <u>An Expository Dictionary of New Testament Words</u> (Old Tappan, New Jersey: Fleming H. Revell Company, 1966), IV, 123.

4   Boettner, pp. 255-258, Godet, pp. 269-271.

5   <u>Ibid</u>.

Another common misconception concerning this passage is that the Church is in view here. Perhaps this is a good place in our discussion to note the distinction between Jesus' return for His Church and His return to establish His Kingdom. As a pretribulationist, this writer believes that Jesus Christ will return for His Church prior to the events beginning in chapter seven of this book. Without delineating the arguments favoring the pretribulational rapture theory, the following is a brief explanation of what it amounts to. According to the theory, Jesus will return in the clouds of heaven to catch up His Church, to be with Him (I Thessalonians 4:15-17), at a time prior to the seven year period known as the great tribulation. The "rapture" is taken from the Greek word *harpazo* meaning to "snatch or catch away."[6] The theory is based on the belief that, since the Church is not appointed to wrath (I Thessalonians 5:9-11), it must be snatched out from the earth prior to the great outpouring of God's wrath, which will take place during the great tribulation.

This book takes the position that, while Jesus was teaching His disciples on Olivet, He did not address the disciples as representatives of the Church, but as representatives of the nation of Israel. The disciples had very little knowledge concerning the Church at this stage in their walk with the Lord. The Lord had taught them that He would build His Church on the basis of Peter's confession, that He was the Christ , the Son of the living God (Matthew 16:17-19). Jesus had also taught certain principles which were to be applied to the Church (Matthew 18:15-20). Other than these things, however, the Church represented little more to the disciples than a future assembly of those who would be called out by Jesus. They had no concept of a "Church Age," nor had

---

6   Vine, I, 174.

they any idea that the Church would be called the body of Christ, made up of both Jew and Gentile alike. They didn't realize what part the Holy Spirit would play in the lives of those who would make up the Church, nor were they aware of any concept that there would be a separate return of Jesus in the clouds to gather the Church to Himself. The disciples were still viewed as, and viewed themselves as a believing remnant of Israel, trusting in their Messiah for the restoration of David's kingdom, with Jesus as King.

For the reasons stated above, the redemption spoken of in Luke 21:28 should be recognized as the redemption of the nation of Israel, rather than the redemption of individual believers who make up the Church. Jesus was telling the disciples that, when the things which were previously spoken of began to happen, the believing remnant of Israel should, at that time, prepare themselves for the long awaited redemption of the nation. The accounts of Matthew and Mark describe the activity surrounding that redemption. With the redemption of Israel, all the saints of the nation will be gathered for the restoration of the kingdom of David.

Proponents of the Church fulfillment view, such as Robert Gundry and Alexander Reese, dispute the belief that this passage is in reference to the redemption of Israel, by stating that Matthew 24:31 and Mark 13:27 speak of the rapture of the Church. Their interpretation is based upon the use of the words "His elect," which they conclude must be a reference to the Church.[7] Yet, the Church is not the only group of people to be called God's elect. God also refers to the nation of Israel as His chosen [elect] people. Again,

---

7   Robert H. Gundry, <u>The Church and the Tribulation</u> (Grand Rapids, Michigan: Zondervan Publishing House, 1973), pp. 134-139; Alexander Reese, <u>The Approaching Advent of Christ</u> (London: Marshal, Morgan, and Scott, 1937; and reprinted Grand Rapids, Michigan: Grand Rapids International Publications, 1975), p. 142.

for the reasons stated previously, the words, "His elect," as they appear in this text should be understood as the chosen people of Israel, rather than the elect of the Church. The fact that the angels will gather the elect from the farthest part of heaven and earth indicates that the Old Testament saints of Israel, the saints who will die during the tribulation, and those surviving the great tribulation will all be gathered for the inauguration of the King. Regarding the surviving remnant of Israel, the prophet Ezekiel wrote that God will gather them together from out of the nations, and will judge them in the wilderness (Ezekiel 20:33-38). More will be written about this judgment of the remnant as we come to the discussion of this in chapter thirteen.

Jesus is coming for His Church. The apostle Paul writes:

> But I do not want you to be ignorant, brethren, concerning those who have fallen asleep, lest you sorrow as others who have no hope. For if we believe that Jesus died and rose again, even so God will bring with Him those who sleep in Jesus.
>
> For this we say to you by the word of the Lord, that we who are alive and remain until the coming of the Lord will by no means precede those who are asleep. For the Lord Himself will descend from heaven with a shout, with the voice of an archangel, and with the trumpet of God. And the dead in Christ will rise first. Then we who are alive and remain shall be caught up together with them in the clouds to meet the Lord in the air. And thus we shall always be with the Lord. Therefore comfort one another with these words. (I Thessalonians 4:13-18)

This book separates this coming of the Lord from Jesus' return for the redemption of the nation of Israel. When Jesus returns to redeem Israel, the Church will already be with Him. Nonetheless, as those who are a part of the Church, we should understand those things surrounding the return of Christ for the redemption of the nation of Israel.

CHAPTER 12
THE PARABLE OF THE FIG TREE

Jesus had answered all of the disciples' questions by this juncture in the discourse. In chapter six the question of what sign would precede the desolation of Jerusalem and the destruction of the temple was answered. The armies surrounding the city would indicate the imminent destruction of Jerusalem. Chapter eight put forth the *abomination of desolation* as the sign which will indicate the coming of the end of the age. The antichrist will present himself as God within the temple of God. In chapter ten heavenly and earthly disturbances were set forth as an indication of the soon return of the Messiah. The sign of the Son of Man was introduced in chapter eleven. This chapter will discuss the question behind the disciples' questions, "When will the Kingdom come?" Jesus knew that His disciples were anxious to know when His Kingdom would be established. Therefore He used a parable to illustrate the nearness of the time for the Kingdom's arrival. The following is the parable of the fig tree and all the other trees:

Now learn this parable from the fig tree: Look at the fig tree and all the trees. When its branch has already become tender and puts forth leaves; *and* when they are already budding, you see and know for yourselves that summer is now near. So you also, when you see these things happening know that the kingdom of God is near, at the *very* doors. Assuredly, I say to you, this generation will by no means pass away until all these things are fulfilled. Heaven and earth will pass away, but my words will by no means pass away. (Matthew 24: 32-35, Mark 13:28-31, Luke 21: 29-33)

There is little difficulty in recognizing that Jesus uses figurative speech here. He states that fact outright: "Now learn this parable …" (Matthew 24:32; Mark 13:28). Not only does He present the parable, but Jesus also gives its interpretation: the budding forecasts the approach of summer, in the same way as the previously indicated signs show that the kingdom of God is very near. While the fig tree may be used as a type of the nation of Israel and all the others trees as types of the other nations, we must be careful not to make the parable say more than what it is intended to say. For example E. Schuyler English calls the fig tree a type of the nation of Israel's bareness, and its budding a sign of the regathering of Israel as a nation.[1] While the fig tree may be considered a type of Israel and the fact that it is without fruit as a type of bareness, the budding as a type of the regathering of the nation poses a problem, especially in light of Luke 21:29, which includes all the other trees. Scripture tells us that Israel will be regathered as a nation, but Scripture does not support the idea that all

---

1   E. Schuyler English, <u>Studies in the Gospel According to Matthew</u> (New York: Fleming H. Revell, 1935), pp. 178-179.

the other nations will be regathered. Bernard Ramm, in his rules for interpreting parables, makes a valid point when he says, "Don't make a parable walk on all fours."[2] Jesus has adequately interpreted this parable within the discourse. There is no need to read any more into the parable than what Jesus has already said.

The words "this generation" in Matthew 24:34, Mark 13:30, and Luke 21:32, have been a source of contention among the various views of this discourse. The proponents of a historical fulfillment of the discourse view these words as proof that the discourse, up to this point, must have been fulfilled within 30 to 100 years following Jesus' proclamation of the discourse.[3] Their argument states that, since all these things must be fulfilled before the passing of this generation, there are only 30 to 100 years in which they must occur. They make two assumptions which must be considered here, which could alter their conclusion. First they assume that "this generation," of which Jesus is speaking, is the generation of the disciples to whom He is addressing the discourse. Secondly, they assume that the word for generation should always be interpreted as a period of 30 to 100 years.

Since the assumptions made under the historical fulfillment view lead to the allegorization of the previous passages, we need to realize that these assumptions are not necessarily true. John Walvoord gives three plausible alternatives to the understanding of the words "this generation." The first two alternatives are based upon other possible translations for the Greek word *genea* translated as generation. This word does not always have to refer to a

2 Bernard Ramm, <u>Protestant Biblical Interpretation</u> (Boston: W.A. Wilde Company, 1950), p.181.
3 Loraine Boettner, <u>The Millenium</u> (Grand Rapids, Michigan: Baker Book House, 1959), p.254.

period of time, but can also be used in reference to a "race" or "nation" of people possessing similar characteristics. Using this translation, Jesus may have been referring to the fact that there would be a perpetuation of the remnant of the nation of Israel. The second alternative meaning for *genea* is the word "age." Were this the meaning that Jesus wanted to convey, then He would have been simply reiterating that the present age would not be completed until all of the signs were fulfilled. The third possibility, which Walvoord prefers, allows the word used for "generation" to be translated according to its usual meaning of 30 to 100 years. This alternative states that instead of the generation of the disciples, Jesus was speaking of the generation of those living during the times described in the previous passages.[4] This would cover the passages between chapters seven and eleven of this book. All three of these interpretations are not only plausible, but they are also consistent with what the rest of the Scriptures teach. This writer is prone to agree with Walvoord's preference for the interpretation of the word *genea* in this passage.

Another reason for maintaining that "this generation" is in some way connected to the end of the age, rather than the generation of the disciples, is found in the context following these words. The words "Heaven and earth will pass away …" are by no means directly related to the events of the first century. The book of the Revelation, however, does connect the events surrounding the end of the age with the passing of heaven and earth (Revelation 21:1). From the context, Jesus doesn't appear to have just interjected a parenthetical thought to His teaching. Rather, He seems to be drawing everything together, and summarizing them by stating, "My words will by no means pass away." The signs

---

4   John F. Walvoord, "Christ's Olivet Discourse on the Time of the End," <u>Bibliotheca Sacra</u>, 129 (January, 1972), 24.

have been told, and, even though heaven and earth will pass away, everything which Jesus has spoken to His disciples will come to pass. His words are true and faithful, and they will remain forever.

The message in this passage is to discern the times. From a pretribulational perspective there are no signs to be fulfilled prior to our Lord's coming for His Church. From the perspective of those who remain behind after the rapture, several events must take place prior to Christ's return to restore the kingdom of David. Jerusalem has to return as the soul possession of Israel. The temple must be rebuilt. The institution of the daily sacrifice needs to be restored. The Antichrist must make a covenant with the nation of Israel. He then must be involved in the *abomination of desolation* as spoken of by the prophet Daniel. He must break His covenant with Israel. The nations must gather together to fight against Jerusalem. There will be a carrying sway of the people into captivity. There will be signs in the heaven and on earth, a great shaking as it were. The sign of the Son of Man will be seen in heaven. The nations of the earth will mourn at His coming. All of these things, and others, must take place before the second coming of our Lord to the earth for the restoration of the kingdom of Israel.

As Christians we need to discern our times. We must be aware of where God is at work and then join in on that work. God has prepared good works for us to walk in. Let us take hold of that which God has prepared for us. We need to ask the question, "Do we see any of the events described in the last paragraph on the horizon?" If we do, perhaps the time of Christ's return for His Church is nearer than we once thought. In the meantime, it is our responsibility to stand fast and be awake. Watch, for the day of the Lord's return is approaching. The time is in the Father's hands, but we know that Jesus is coming.

CHAPTER 13
JUDGMENT FOR ISRAEL

After telling the parable of the fig tree and all the other trees, Jesus related a passage of judgment in relationship to His return. This writer believes that this judgment will come upon those who remain of the nation of Israel after the great tribulation. The following is the prediction of this judgment which will come with the coming of the Son of Man:

> But of that day and that hour no one knows, no, not even the angels, nor the Son, but My Father only. But as the days of Noah *were*, so also will the coming of the Son of Man be. For as in the days before the flood, they were eating and drinking, marrying and giving in marriage, until the flood came and took them all away, so also will the coming of the Son of Man be. Then two *men* will be in the field: one will be taken and the other left. Two *women will* be grinding at the mill: one will be taken and the other left. Watch therefore, for you do not know what hour our Lord is coming. Take heed, watch

and pray; for you do not know when the time is.
(Matthew 24:36-42, Mark 13: 32-33)

Though there will be signs to indicate the approach of the end of the age and Jesus' return, the exact time of that return is something that is known by the Father alone. Once again, Jesus sets forth the immanency of His return, by declaring that those who are watching may be able to know the signs of His return, but no one, except the Father, knows the exact time of that return. The words "nor the Son" present a rather interesting theological question. "If God is omniscient [which He is], and Jesus is God [which He is], then how is it that there is something which the Son does not know?" Without being overly simplistic, the answer to this question can be seen in the *kenosis* passage (Philippians 2:5-11). Since Jesus could lay aside His glory to become a servant fashioned in the likeness of man, then He can also lay aside His knowledge of the time of His return, leaving that knowledge in the Father's authority (Acts 1:7). How this is accomplished is a matter, which this writer believes, must also be left in God's hands. As the psalmist David wrote:

> Lord, my heart is not haughty,
> Nor my eyes lofty,
> Neither do I concern myself with great matters,
> Nor with things too profound for me. (Psalm 131:1)

Jesus, in speaking of His return, compared it to the flood in the days of Noah. That flood was a judgment on the whole world. Care should be taken, in making a proper interpretation of this, to avoid carrying the comparison further than what is suggested in the text. In this case, there are two similarities in view, normal daily activities of life, and a taking away. The question which needs to be answered then is, "In what ways do these two things relate to the flood in Noah's day?"

The eating and drinking, marrying and giving in marriage, all represent the normal routine of life which was taking place, while Noah was building the ark. God had seen the corruption of men's hearts and had announced the coming judgment to Noah. Genesis 6:3 indicates that the Spirit of God strove with men during this time prior to the flood, but mankind, with the exception of Noah and his family, ignored the warning of impending judgment. Thus, what Jesus was implying here is that even though God had warned of impending judgment, mankind had become so calloused in heart that the warning went out as to a deaf audience. In the first letter to the Thessalonians Paul wrote that the day of the Lord will come as a thief in the night (I Thessalonians 5:2). The point that Paul made and that Jesus makes is that, even though God has warned of this terrible judgment, it will come upon the world at a time when mankind is not expecting it. Moreover, Peter wrote in his second letter that there will be scoffers in the last days, who will completely dismiss the idea of God's judgment, ignoring the fact that God judged the world in the days of Noah by the flood (II Peter 3:3-7).

The second part of the comparison has to do with a taking away. Jesus spoke of the flood, saying that it "came and took them all away" (Matthew 24:39). From the context the "all" of this phrase is indicating all of those people who were carrying on normal activities, while ignoring God's warning of judgment. There were only eight people saved through the flood: Noah, his wife, his three sons, and their wives. However, while the rest of the world was carrying on normal activities, Noah was building the ark, preparing for the upcoming judgment. Yet, those who were taken away, according to this passage, were those who were swept away by the flood because they were not prepared. This is the picture which must be carried over into Jesus' comparison of a future taking away. This picture is also consistent with the admonition to watch which follows the comparison.

Proponents of a Church fulfillment view of this discourse, such as Robert Gundry and Alexander Reese, have concluded that the taking away of this passage represents the rapture of the Church.[1] This writer believes that the Church will be raptured, but that the rapture will occur before the great tribulation, rather than at the end of the age. Along side of the previously stated argument that the disciples were not representative of the Church, there exists another reason why the conclusion reached by Gundry and Reese is inconsistent with the context of this passage. The rapture is an event where believers in Jesus Christ, who are awaiting Jesus' return, are gathered together to be with the Lord. The taking away described in this passage is one which is associated with those who were swept away by the flood, because they ignored the warning. Had Jesus' comparison been with Noah and his family, then the rapture might stand as a valid comparison. However, Jesus didn't make the comparison to those who were saved, but with those who perished in the flood.

We have concluded that the comparison is associated with judgment. The question arises, however, as to which judgment Jesus is referring. The Scriptures seem to indicate that there are four future major judgments which are associated with the last days. They are: 1. the judgment of the Church, sometimes referred to as the Bema Seat judgment (Romans 14:10; I Corinthians 3:11-15; II Corinthians 5:10),

---

1   Robert H. Gundry, The Church and the Tribulation (Grand Rapids, Michigan: Zondervan Publishing House, 1973) pp.137-139; Alexander Reese, The Approaching Advent of Christ (London: Marshal, Morgan, and Scott, 1975), p. 29.

2. The judgment of the nation of Israel (Ezekiel 20:33-44; Malachi 3:2-6), 3. The judgment of the Gentile nations (Joel 3:2, Matthew 25:31-46; et al), and 4. The final judgment of the wicked dead, also called the Great White Throne judgment (Revelation 20:11-16).

This writer believes that the judgment which Jesus has in mind at this juncture of the discourse is the judgment of the nation of Israel. The Bema Seat and Great White Throne judgments take place in heaven, whereas this judgment appears to take place on earth. The remaining possible choices include the judgment of the Gentiles and the judgment of Israel. Since Jesus is speaking to His disciples, who are representative of the remnant of the nation Israel, the judgment of Israel becomes the most plausible choice of the four major judgments.

Moreover, this writer believes that the judgment of Israel will take place in the forty-five days prior to the restoration of the Kingdom. In Daniel chapter twelve, Daniel mentions that, "Blessed is he who waits, and comes to the one thousand three hundred and thirty-five days." (Daniel 12:12). Blessing is reserved in Scripture for those who have a right relationship with God. Therefore, this writer believes that this blessing is for the saved of Israel, from the great tribulation, which will enter into the Kingdom of Jesus Christ.

The prophets Ezekiel and Malachi describe a purging of the nation of Israel in the days prior to the restoration of Israel. Through this purging process God will eliminate those who rebel against His authority and profane His name from those who will enter into the reestablished Kingdom. Malachi compares this judgment to the refiner's fire or the fuller's soap (Malachi 3:2-3). Ezekiel, on the other hand, describes the judgment like a shepherd who makes his sheep pass under the rod before entering the fold (Ezekiel 20:37-38). The following is what Ezekiel prophesied:

"I will make you pass under the rod, and I will bring you into the bond of the covenant; I will purge the rebels from among you, and those who transgress against Me; I will bring them out of the country where they dwell, but they shall not enter the land of Israel. Then you will know that I *am* the LORD. (Ezekiel 20:37-38)

In both Malachi and Ezekiel, those who will enter into the restored Kingdom will be those who willingly desire to serve the LORD their God. In Ezekiel, the Lord makes it abundantly clear that those who will enter in will not do so on the merits of their own righteousness. In fact, they will loathe themselves because of the evil which they have committed. (Ezekiel 20:43-44).

As we look back over the previous two chapters and this chapter, we see the sign, the parable, and the warning surrounding the coming of the Son of Man are all directed toward the believing remnant of Israel, who will be present during the last days of the great tribulation. The exact time of Christ's return is purposely left indefinite. Only the Father knows when that will be. In light of this fact, Jesus admonishes those who will read this during these latter days to watch and pray. Those who are watching will know that the time for Christ's return is approaching and those who pray will be kept from the snares of Satan, as he goes about to deceive the whole world.

Though this portion is addressed primarily to the tribulation saints, the principles nonetheless apply to us today. The tribulation saints are told to perceive the signs of the time that they may realize that the Kingdom is close at hand. Today, we, too, should be watchful and observe the signs of the times, signs which are precursors of things to come. The Lord Jesus Christ is coming to take His Church to be with Him, and the closer we draw to the end of the age, the nearer the rapture of the Church will be. The reason why many in Israel will be unprepared for the Lord's arrival will be because they are too caught up in normal daily affairs of life. The reason why many Christians are not effective in the Lord's work is that they too are so caught up in the daily affairs of life that they don't have time to be involved in ministry for Jesus. The time for the Lord's return is drawing nearer, and whether it be the Church at the Bema seat (Romans 14:10) or Israel in the wilderness (Ezekiel 20:35), there is going to be a purging. For believers in the Church, there will be no expulsion from the Kingdom, but some will suffer loss, and, yet, be saved as through fire (I Corinthians 3:15).

In the chapters which will follow, Jesus changes from direct teaching to teaching by parables. He teaches through a series of parables which appear to be directed at various audiences. Some appear to be directed at the disciples and those that will follow them. Another appears to be directed at the nation of Israel. And, yet, another appears to be directed to the world in general. Following the parables is the final passage of the discourse, which deals with the judgment of the Gentiles.

Parables of Readiness

Part I

Chapter 14
The Master and His Household

As Jesus began teaching His disciples on the slope of Olivet, He answered their questions regarding the demise of Jerusalem, the end of the age, and His return, but, more importantly, Jesus focused the disciples' attention to matters of greater concern. The disciples were anxious to know the signs which would forecast the approach of Christ's Kingdom. They had heard much about the Kingdom, as they walked with Jesus, and they knew that they would have a role alongside of Jesus during His reign (Matthew 19:27-30). So, they eagerly anticipated the arrival of the Kingdom, and the part that they would have in it. The Lord, however, wanted them to understand that the end would not come immediately, and that many disturbing events would take place before that time. He warned of deceptions which would have the effect of leading many astray, because of their eagerness to see the Messiah upon His return. Moreover, Jesus emphasized that the gospel of the Kingdom must be preached to every nation before the end of the age will come.

The first set of parables seems to focus on the disciples and their followers, who would become the Church. The following is a composite of these parables:

> But know this, that if the master of the house had known what hour the thief would come, he would have watched and not allowed his house to be broken into. Therefore you also be ready, for the Son of Man is coming at an hour when you do not expect Him. (Matthew 24:43-44)
>
> It is like a man going to a far country, who left his house and gave authority to his servants, and to each his work, and commanded the doorkeeper to watch. Watch therefore, for you do not know when the master of the house is coming--in the evening, at midnight, at the crowing of the rooster, or in the morning--lest, coming suddenly, he find you sleeping. And what I say to you, I say to all: Watch_ (Mark 13:34-37)
>
> Who is a faithful and wise servant, whom his master made ruler over his household, to give food in due season? Blessed is that servant whom his master, when he comes, will find so doing. Assuredly, I say unto you that he will make him ruler over all his goods. But if that evil servant says in his heart, "My master is delaying his coming," and begins to beat his fellow servants, and to eat and drink with drunkards, the master of that servant will come on a day when he is not looking for him and at an hour that he is not aware of, and will cut him in two and appoint him his portion with the hypocrites. There

shall be weeping and gnashing of teeth. (Matthew 24:45-51)

But take heed to yourselves, lest your hearts be weighed down with carousing, drunkenness, and cares of this life, and that Day come on you unexpectedly. For it will come as a snare on all those who dwell on the face of the whole earth. Watch, therefore, and pray that you may be counted worthy to escape all these things that will come to pass, and to stand before the Son of Man. (Luke 21:34-36)

The motif of this set of parables is that of a householder and his household. To begin this set of parables, Jesus points out that the householder, himself, would have be on the lookout to prevent his house from being broken into by a thief, if he had known when the thief was coming. The emphasis here is the necessity of watchfulness and readiness for an unexpected event. Jesus is not trying to compare himself to a common thief, who comes to rob, disrupt, and destroy. Rather, He points out that His return will come unexpectedly, just as the thief is unexpected. If the owner of the house had been aware that a thief was coming, he would have prepared in advance to prevent his house from being broken into. In a similar manner the disciples and their followers should be prepared for the Lord's return, at a time when He is not expected. Since the Lord's return for His Church could be at any time, this requires constant vigilance and readiness for Jesus' return.

The second comparison that Jesus makes is to a householder who goes away and leaves a servant in charge as a doorkeeper. In this parable Jesus compares Himself with the master of the house, and His disciples are compared to the doorkeeper. The master goes away and gives charge to his doorkeeper to keep watch over the household. The last thing that the master would expect would be to return and find the doorkeeper sleeping. Such a doorkeeper would have neglected the command he had been given to watch. In the same way, we, as believers in the Lord Jesus Christ, can neglect the responsibility we have been given to spread the good news of the Kingdom. The disciples had been taught by the Master and they would be charged by the Master with a commission, prior to His ascension into heaven (Matthew 28:18-20). Jesus told His disciples to watch, but He carried that command even further. This responsibility goes further than to just the disciples, the command goes to all who read this message. Jesus closed this parable with a one word command, "Watch_"

Clearly, this command is applicable to the Church today. The signs of our times indicate that the Lord could return for His Church at any moment. We are to be alert to that probability. If, on the other hand, we, who have been given the responsibility to watch, neglect to recognize the immanency of our Lord's return and become slothful in our responsibilities, then when the Lord does return, we might well be ashamed at His coming (I John 2:28).

In the next parable, Jesus continues with the servant-master motif. This is quite fitting, since Jesus also, "made Himself of no reputation, taking the form of a servant …" (Philippians 2:7). Moreover, in speaking to His disciples on the subject of greatness, Jesus explained that, in the Kingdom of God, anyone desiring to be first must be "last of all and servant of all" (Mark 10:35). In the days following this discourse, Jesus once again, demonstrated this principle during the upper room discourse, in which He took the form of a servant and washed the feet of the disciples. (John 13:2-17)

In this parable, Jesus illustrated two different types of servants, those who are faithful and wise, and those who are evil. The difference in these servants lies in the manner in which they carry out the responsibilities entrusted to them. The faithful and wise servant carries out the responsibility of providing for the master's household, while the evil servant, thinking that the master will delay his return, begins to act contrary to his master's commands.

Notice first that the responsibility is given to servants who have a place of leadership within the household. Unlike the doorkeeper in the previous parable, who is found to be slothful upon the master's return, the evil servant deliberately acts contrary to his master's command. Jesus says that the evil servant will be appointed a place with the hypocrites. This is because the evil servant had only professed to be the master's servant, but as soon as he thinks that the master is not watching, he turns against his fellow servants and is willfully disobedient to his master. This is like the person who professes to have a relationship with Jesus Christ, but his actions toward his fellow servants and toward the commandments of Christ reveal the fact that he does not have a regenerated heart. He has never received a personal relationship with Christ. He only professes to know Christ for whatever he can get out of that profession. The distinction that is illustrated in this parable is the difference between those who have trusted Jesus Christ as their Lord and Savior, and those who have made a mere profession of knowing Jesus Christ. Jesus, Himself, in the Sermon on the Mount, said:

> Not everyone who says to Me, "Lord, Lord," will enter the kingdom of heaven, but he who does the will of My Father in heaven. Many will say to Me in that day, "Lord, Lord have we not prophesied in Your name, cast out demons in Your name, and done many wonders in Your name. And then I will declare

to them, "I never knew you, depart from Me, you
who practice lawlessness_ (Matthew 7:21-23)

Even among the disciples, there was one who did not know
Jesus, even having walked with Him for nearly three and a
half years. Judas Iscariot had been with the disciples from
nearly the beginning of Jesus' earthly ministry, and yet he
only professed to be His follower. Judas' act of betrayal
revealed that he was not a true disciple of Jesus Christ.

Notice that the hypocrite is revealed through his
actions. He, "says in his heart, 'My master is delaying his
coming,' and begins to beat his fellow servants, and to eat
and drink with drunkards" (Matthew 24:48-49). The action
of this evil servant begins in the heart. The evil servant's
heart is not set on doing the master's will. This reveals an
unregenerate heart, a heart that has not been changed by
the love of Jesus. As soon as he is convinced that the master
will not see his evil actions he begins to act contrary to his
master's commands. He begins to beat his fellow servants.
The apostle John wrote, "If someone says, 'I love God,' and
hates his brother, he is a liar ..." (I John 4:20). One way
to recognize a professor from a possessor of a relationship
with Jesus Christ is by his actions toward fellow believers.
A man cannot hate his fellow believers and at the same
time be in a right relationship with Jesus Christ. He has
either fallen out of fellowship with Christ or, worse yet,
never had a relationship with Him to begin with. Moreover,
this evil servant begins to associate with those who mock a
relationship with God, those who willfully follow the ways
of the world and shun the ways of God. The professing
Christian can only play the part of a faithful servant for a
while. Sooner or later, because he has a non-regenerate heart,
his sinful nature will lead him to believe that God will not
see his rebellion, and he will return to his sinful life style.

The faithful and wise servant will obey, from the heart, his master's commands to feed the household of faith. His focus will be on doing that which pleases his master. In opposition to this, the evil servant is looking to what he can get out of pretending to be the master's servant. He cannot keep up his pretense forever, and his actions will reveal the nature of his heart. Many have professed to know Jesus with noble intentions, but because they do not have a personal relationship with Him, their noble intentions become filthy rags, and they dishonor the One whom they profess to believe in.

This parable stands as an admonition to all those who come under the hearing of Christ's teaching to examine their hearts. Are you following Christ because you understand what He has done on your behalf and you are therefore grateful for His finished work? Do you serve Him because you love Him? Or, are you serving Jesus because you think there is something to gain by professing to know Him? These are matters of the heart, and can only be answered by the individual himself or herself. There are many who attend churches today, who have listened to words of the Lord, and yet have not obeyed from the heart His command to place their faith in Himself as Savior and Lord. Many of these claim that they are Christians, but the day will come when, if they do not repent, they will stand before the Lord and He will say, "Depart from Me, I never knew you_" Now is the time to examine your own heart. Is it the heart of a faithful and wise servant, or does it resemble the heart of the evil servant.

The evil servant is clearly an unbeliever, since Jesus says that He will cut him in two and appoint him a place with the hypocrites. Moreover, Jesus says that there will be weeping and gnashing of teeth. These are things which are reserved for unbelievers and not for those who have trusted in Christ as their Savior. Today is the day of salvation. If your heart isn't right with Jesus, He is waiting for you to come to Him and have a relationship with Him. Don't wait. Watch_ What this writer writes to you is also what he writes to himself.

The final paragraph of this section is not a parable, but a fitting admonition in light of the parables that have preceded it. Jesus admonishes his disciples and their followers to keep a watch over their own hearts. The carousing, drunkenness, and cares of this life are given as indications of being turned from a watchful servant to one who will be caught unexpectedly. This paragraph, however, doesn't appear to be making the same distinction between believers and professing non-believers which were made in the previous parable. This is more of an admonition to believers, in light of what the previous parable had to say. This paragraph ends with an admonition to the disciples to watch and pray that they might escape the tribulation which is coming upon the whole world and to be able to stand before the Lord. Non-believers will not be able to stand before the Lord.

Allow one final note of comparison before we move on to the next parable. The master in the last parable of this section is master of both the faithful and the evil servants. Whether the world wishes to acknowledge this fact or not, Jesus Christ is Lord of all. A day is coming for which God has decreed, "that at the name of Jesus every knee should bow, of those in heaven, and of those on earth, and of those under the earth, and that every tongue should confess that Jesus Christ is Lord, to the glory of God the Father" (Philippians 2:10-11). Jesus is Lord_

PARABLES OF READINESS

PART 2

CHAPTER 15
THE TEN VIRGINS

In the opening passages of the Olivet Discourse, Jesus addressed His disciples directly. He told them things which would be helpful to them in the days and years following His departure. After Jesus had delineated the demise of Jerusalem, however, He changed the audience that He was addressing. Jesus began to speak to those who would be alive during the Tribulation period. The majority of those passages were directed to the believing remnant of the nation of Israel who would experience the horrible events of the great tribulation.

The next parable changes motif which indicates a change in the audience Jesus intends to reach with the parable. This parable employs the use of a portion of the Jewish wedding ceremony. Both this parable and the one following it are found only in the book of Matthew. The following is the parable which Jesus taught with regard to the wise and the foolish virgins:

Then the kingdom of heaven shall be likened to ten virgins who took their lamps and went out to meet the bridegroom. Now five of them were wise, and five were foolish. Those who were foolish took their lamps and took no oil with them, but the wise took oil in their vessels with their lamps. But while the bridegroom was delayed, they all slumbered and slept. And at midnight a cry was heard: "Behold the bridegroom is coming; go out and meet him_" Then all those virgins arose and trimmed their lamps. And the foolish said to the wise, "Give us some of your oil, for our lamps are going out." But the wise answered saying, "No, lest there should not be enough for us and you; but go rather to those who sell, and buy for yourselves." And while they went to buy, the bridegroom came, and those who were ready went in with him to the wedding; and the door was shut. Afterward the other virgins came also saying, "Lord, lord open to us_" But he answered and said, "Assuredly I say to you, I do not know you." Watch therefore, for you know neither the day nor the hour in which the Son of Man is coming. (Matthew 25: 1-13)

The motif in this parable suggests that Jesus was directing this parable to a select group of people. This writer believes that the group which Jesus aimed this parable is the Jewish people who will be looking for His coming at the end of the tribulation period. In the marriage ceremony, it was customary for the bridegroom and his party to go to the bride's home and bring the bride to the bridegroom's father's home for the wedding festivities. Friends of the couple would

join in the wedding procession leading to the father's home.[1]
As this parable is presented, the ten virgins would seem to be
friends of the couple, and they were waiting for the arrival
of the bridegroom so that they could join in the joyous
occasion. These ten virgins, most likely, represent members
of the nation of Israel as they anticipate the coming of
Messiah.

The virgins had all taken their lamps and were waiting
in an appropriate place to meet the wedding party. However,
five of the virgins had not counted on a delay in the
bridegroom's coming, which resulted in his coming during
the night. They had failed to prepare for that eventuality.
The result was that they were unprepared at the time of
his coming, and, therefore, had to leave, in order to buy
oil. By the time they were able to return, they were shut
out of the festivities altogether. The bridegroom's response
is reminiscent of Jesus' words during the Sermon on the
Mount. (see Matthew 7:23)

Once again, we could make this parable say many
things by taking into account the various types which may
be represented herein. For example the bridegroom could be
used as a type of the King, since the bridegroom was treated
as a king in the Jewish wedding ceremony during the week
of the wedding.[2] The lamps and the oil could also be seen as
types of the Holy Spirit present in human vessels. Jesus had
also spoken of His followers as being lamps (Matthew 5:13-
15). Yet the rule remains, "Don't make a parable walk on all
fours." A parable is intended to teach a singular principle, and

---

1   Ray E. Baughman, <u>The Life of Christ Visualized</u> (Chicago: The
Moody Bible Institute, 1968), p. 233.

2   <u>The Zondervan Pictorial Encyclopedia of the Bible</u>, Merrill C.
Tenney, gen. edit. (Grand Rapids: Zondervan Publishing House,
1982), IV, 97.

not a myriad of details. Therefore we need to concentrate on the principle being taught in this parable.

The foolish virgins neglected to prepare themselves for the coming of the bridegroom, in the way that they should have. They had their lamps and they had gathered in the right place, but they didn't have the oil which was needed for the lamps. Apparently, they considered the things which they had done to be sufficient preparation for the coming festivities. Their actions, upon news of the bridegroom's arrival, suggest that they may have neglected to purchase oil, because they felt they could rely on the preparations made by the wise virgins to carry them along. Again, the fact that they went to purchase the oil and returned expecting to receive admittance, may also suggest that they felt that they could prepare themselves in the last minutes, prior to the bridegroom's arrival. The bridegroom's response to their request for entry shows that, as far as the bridegroom was concerned, only those who were prepared for his coming were to be recognized as guests for his wedding.

If indeed this parable is directed toward the people of the nation of Israel in the last days, then the principle demonstrated in this passage is that those who expect to be received by the King are going to have to rely on more than the facts that they are Israelites and that they have a knowledge of the King's coming. The King will expect that they will have had a relationship with Him by faith. Moreover, they will not be able to rely on the faith of their neighbors or relatives to carry them into the Kingdom. Once Jesus comes, it will be too late to make the needed preparation. They will be shut out of the Kingdom.

Though this parable may be directed toward the nation of Israel in the end times, as this writer believes it is. Many today are relying on insufficient preparation for the coming of our Lord Jesus Christ. Some believe that because they have become members of a certain local church, then that qualifies them for entrance into Christ's Kingdom. Others believe that because their parents have received Christ as their personal Savior, then that is all that is necessary to make them Christians. Still others have taken the position, that, when the time comes, there will be plenty of time to do what is needed to prepare for the King. These are all like the foolish virgins. The only way to be prepared for the Lord's coming is by having a personal relationship with the King Himself, by grace through faith. Jesus is the only door into the Kingdom. Just owning a Bible, or being a member of a local church, or having Christian parents, or going to Sunday school will not qualify someone for the Kingdom of God. As for those who believe that they can wait until the final hour, they have no idea when that hour will be. As Jesus has already warned, His return will come to the unprepared, at an hour when they are not expecting it.

How foolish it is for those who wait. And, how foolish it is, for those relying on the wrong things for salvation, when all that Jesus requires is that one have a personal relationship with Him, by faith in His finished work. Jesus came the first time to die for the sins of the whole world (I John 2:2). The penalty for sin is death [eternal separation from God] (Romans 6:23), and Jesus alone could pay that penalty for sinners, because He alone is sinless. Yet, not only did He die to pay that penalty, but He also lives to offer His own righteousness to those who will receive Him by faith (Romans 3:21-26). Jesus died for our sins and lives to offer us eternal life through faith in Him (I Corinthians 15:1-4). If you haven't received Jesus as your own personal Savior by faith, don't wait_

For He says:

"In an acceptable time I have heard
you.

And in the day of salvation I have
helped you."

Behold, now is the accepted time; behold, now is the day of salvation (II Corinthians 6:2).

PARABLES OF READINESS

PART 3

CHAPTER 16
THE PROFITABLE AND UNPROFITABLE SERVANTS

Though the majority of the Olivet Discourse is focused primarily on a remnant of the nation of Israel living during the Tribulation Period, we need to remember that the tribulation is a world-wide event. The book of the Revelation depicts catastrophic events which take place on world-wide scale. This last parable seems to be directed to a world-wide audience. Most likely it is directed to those living on the earth during the Tribulation Period, but it clearly has implications for our present age as well.

Like the parables at the beginning of this section, the motif of this final parable is that of the servant-master relationship. As with the other servant parables, the master goes away leaving the servants in charge of something until he should return. In this particular case, the expectation of the master is that he should receive a profit, upon his return, from the talents which he has entrusted to his servants. The following is the parable of the profitable and unprofitable servants:

> For the kingdom of heaven is like a man traveling to a far country, who called his own servants and delivered his goods to them. And to one he gave five talents, to another two, and to another one, to each according to his own ability; and immediately he went on a journey. Then he who had received the five talents went and traded them, and made another five talents. And likewise he who received two gained two more also. But he who had received one went and dug in the ground, and hid his lord's money. (Matthew 25:14-18)
>
> After a long time the lord of those servants came and settled accounts with them. So he who had received five talents came and brought five other talents, saying, "Lord you delivered to me five talents; look, I have gained five more talents besides them." His lord said to him, "Well done, good and faithful servant; you were faithful over a few things, I will make you ruler over many things. Enter into the joy of your lord." (Matthew 25:19-21)
>
> He also who had received two talents came and said, "Lord, you delivered to me two talents; look, I have gained two more talents besides them." His lord said to him, "Well done, good and faithful servant: you have been faithful over a few things, I will make you ruler over many things. Enter into the joy of your lord." (Matthew 25:22-23)
>
> Then he who had received the one talent came and said, "Lord, I knew you to be a hard man, reaping where you have not sown, and gathering where you

have not scattered seed. And I was afraid, and went out and hid your talent in the ground. Look, there you have what is yours." But the Lord answered and said to him, "You wicked and lazy servant, you knew that I reap where I have not sown, and gather where I did not scatter seed. Therefore you ought to have deposited my money with the bankers, and at my coming I would have received back my own with interest. Therefore take the talent from him and give it to him who has ten talents. For to everyone who has, more will be given, and he will have abundance; but from him who does not have, even what he has will be taken away. And cast the unprofitable servant into outer darkness. There will be weeping and gnashing of teeth." (Matthew 25: 24-30)

Before the traveling man goes on his journey, he entrusts a certain amount of His wealth to his servants. Notice particularly, that each servant was given "according to his own ability." This statement indicates, early in the parable, that the master was expecting something to be done with the amounts being distributed. Yet, the statement also tells us that the master was not expecting anything more of the servants than what they were capable of accomplishing. Jesus had added in an earlier parable of this nature, "For everyone to whom much is given, from him much will be required, and to whom much has been committed, of him they will ask the more" (Luke 12:48). The point being made, however, is that there is a responsibility to do something with the talents which are given.

The talent spoken of in this parable, is not what we would commonly think of today as being a talent, but it is a measure of either gold or silver, and it was equivalent to approximately three thousand days wages.[1] The modern meaning of "talent" was derived from its original meaning of "something weighed," as influenced by this parable. Thus, a talent is viewed as something which God has weighed out to someone, such as an ability or gift.[2] The parable demonstrates that the master was not as much concerned with what was done with his money, as he was with what each servant did with the ability that he possessed. Both he who was given the five talents and he who was given the two talents were rewarded with the same words of tribute, "Well done, good and faithful servant, you have been faithful over a few things, I will make you ruler over many things. Enter into the joy of your lord" (Matthew 25:21, 23).

In making the comparison between this parable and the Kingdom of God, we must examine what it is that Jesus gives to individuals. Perhaps the single most important thing which Jesus has given to His disciples and to us, as a result of His earthly ministry, is the message of the Kingdom of heaven. The one thing which Jesus emphasized, in the beginning of this discourse, which must occur before the end will come, is that the message of the Kingdom must be preached throughout the world. The point that Jesus made while describing the persecutions that His disciples would undergo was that, through their trials the gospel would be preached to all nations. Jesus gave His disciples the good news of the Kingdom and that good news has been passed down through the centuries since then. That message spread and will spread throughout the world. The responsibility which Jesus gave to His disciples and to all

---

1   The Zondervan Pictorial Encyclopedia of the Bible, Merrill C. Tenney, gen. ed. (Grand Rapids: Zonervan Publishing House, 1982), V, 920.

2   W.E. Vine, Expository Dictionary of New Testament Words, (Old Tappan, New Jersey: The Fleming H. Revell Co., 1966), IV, 108.

who will receive His message of the Kingdom is to spread that message throughout the world.

The unprofitable servant received the talent from his master, and knew that his master would require it of him upon his return. Yet, though he understood that his master would expect more than what was given, he decided to hide the talent and go about life as usual until the master returned. The servant didn't put the ability which he possessed to use in order to bring a profit to the gift which had been entrusted to him by the master. The end result was that the servant lost even that which had been given to him, and he, himself, was cast into outer darkness. Again, the weeping and gnashing of teeth indicate that the unprofitable servant is representative of those who will not enter into the Kingdom.

This writer believes that this parable is directed, primarily, to those who will hear of the coming Kingdom during the last days, but that the principle being taught goes beyond that generation to everyone. There are some today like the unprofitable servant. They have heard the good news of salvation that is through faith in Jesus Christ, but, like the unprofitable servant, they have done nothing with that message. They have hidden it, and have continued living their lives in the manner to which they have been accustomed. They know that God will one day exact judgment, but they have deceived themselves into thinking that all that will be required of them is to have heard the Word.

The master calls the unprofitable servant both lazy and wicked: lazy, because, even though he had the ability to do something with the talent, he chose to do nothing, and wicked, because he knew the truth about the master, but chose to act in a way that was contradictory to what he knew. Those who have heard the gospel of Jesus Christ, and have not responded, are no different than that lazy and wicked servant. They have heard the Word and all that Jesus requires of them is that they receive Him by faith. Jesus does not expect any more of us than what we have the ability to do. Yet, some chose to do nothing. Moreover, they know the truth, and because they choose to do nothing, they are, in fact, choosing to disobey the truth.

This writer remembers seeing a gospel tract which had something written on the front, in words to the effect of, "What do you have to do in order to be eternally lost?" Inside the tract, the middle pages were blank. The point was very clear; one needs to do "nothing" in order to be eternally separated from God. Yet, how tragic it is, for someone to have heard the words of eternal life, and to do nothing. The gift is free (Romans 6:23). Jesus paid the awful price for our salvation. All that is required is that it be received by faith. Have you accepted Jesus Christ as your personal Savior by faith? If not, why not? Those who ignore the truth are no different than the unprofitable servant.

Chapter 17
The Judgment of the Sheep and Goats

Once Jesus had made it perfectly clear that everyone should be ready for His return, He described one last matter which will take place prior to the establishment of His earthly Kingdom. As Jesus closed out the Olivet discourse, He presented to His disciples a glimpse of His final act of judgment, prior to the establishment of His earthly Kingdom. The following is the scene which Jesus revealed to His disciples:

> When the Son of man comes in His glory, and all the angels with Him, then He will sit on the throne of His glory. All the nations will be gathered before Him, and He will separate them one from another, as a shepherd divides his sheep from the goats. And He will set the sheep on His right hand, but the goats on the left. (Matthew 25:31-33)
>
> Then the King will say to those on His right hand, "Come, you blessed of My Father, inherit the kingdom prepared for you from the foundation o the world: for I was hungry and you gave Me

food; I was thirsty and you gave Me drink; I was a stranger and you took Me in; I was naked and you clothed Me; I was sick and you visited Me; I was in prison and you came to Me." Then the righteous will answer Him saying, "Lord, when did we see You hungry and feed You, or thirsty and give You drink? When did we see You a stranger and take You in, or naked and clothe You? Or when did we see you sick, or in prison, and come to you?" And the King will answer and say to them, "Assuredly, I say to you, inasmuch as you did it to one of the least of these My brethren, you did it to Me." (Matthew 25:34-40)

Then He will also say to those on the left hand, "Depart from Me, you cursed, into the everlasting fire prepared for the devil and his angels: for I was hungry and you gave Me no food; I was thirsty and you gave Me no drink; I was a stranger and you did not take Me in, naked and you did not clothe Me, sick and in prison and you did not visit Me." Then they will answer Him, saying, "Lord, when did we see you hungry or thirsty or a stranger or naked or sick or in prison, and did not minister to You?" Then He will answer them, saying, "Assuredly, I say to you, inasmuch as you did not do it to the least of these, you did not it to Me." And these will go into everlasting punishment, but the righteous into eternal life. (Matthew 25: 41-46)

This scene opens with the Son of Man coming in His glory to be seated on His glorious throne. That raises the question, "Coming from where and to where?" To answer this question, we need to go back the disciples' inquiries and realize that their expectation was that Jesus would leave

Jerusalem and return to Jerusalem. Taking that as a starting point, we can next look into the book of Acts, and see that the place from which Jesus left and the place of His promised return was the Mount of Olives, which is directly across the Kidron Valley and opposite the city of Jerusalem. Jesus had ascended into heaven and was to return to earth, in the same manner in which He left (Acts 1:11). The scene which is depicted here is that of Jesus approaching His throne in Jerusalem, having made His return from heaven to earth (compare with Matthew 24:30). The time will have come for Jesus to reign on the throne of David.

Some proponents of the historical fulfillment position, however, view this scene as synonymous with the judgment at the great white throne depicted in Revelation 20:11.[1] The first obvious distinction between the events described here and the great white throne judgment is that Jesus is returning in glory to earth, while the great white throne judgment depicts the scene of heaven and earth fleeing from the presence of Him who sits on the throne. Secondly, in this scene the nations are gathered before the throne, righteous and unrighteous. At the great white throne, there is only one group gathered before the throne, the dead who have not been previously judged (Revelation 20:11-15). From His glorious throne, Jesus receives some into the Kingdom as their reward, and the rest are sent to everlasting punishment. At the great white throne, all are sent into the lake of fire. The judgment depicted here takes place prior to Jesus' reign on earth. The judgment of the great white throne occurs after Jesus has reigned for a thousand years (see Revelation 20:4-6). These two judgments are vastly different. They happen at different times, in different places, for different purposes, with different people, and before different thrones.

---

1   Roland Q. Leavell, <u>Studies in Matthew: The King and the Kingdom</u> (Nashville, Tennessee: Convention Press, 1962), p. 124.

The nations are separated into two groups as they stand before the throne. The Greek word interpreted here as "nations" is *ethnos* which denotes primarily a multitude, but when it is used in the plural, as it is in this case, the word is used in reference to all other nations outside of Israel.[2] A few commentators have interpreted this to mean national entities, other than Israel, will be separated before Jesus, rather than individuals from out of the nations.[3] Such an interpretation, however, creates an enormous problem. Rarely, if ever, would one find a national entity which would be made up of entirely believers or entirely non-believers. In such a case, believers would be sent to everlasting punishment and non-believers would enjoy entrance into the Kingdom based on their national origin. Moreover, simple observation shows us that national entities are constantly changing. The more that such a view is examined, the more complex the problems become. The conclusion which must be drawn is that Jesus will separate, from out of the nations, believers (righteous) and non-believers (unrighteous).

The purpose of this judgment is to apportion rewards to the group designated as sheep and punishment to the group designated as goats. A distinction must be made here between the basis for the apportioning of rewards and punishments as opposed to the basis for the individuals being assigned to one group or the other. Charles Spurgeon made a valid observation regarding this matter when he wrote, "Our Lord does not mean to teach that men will be condemned because they have not been charitable to the poor and needy or that

---

2   W.E. Vine, <u>Expository Dictionary of New Testament Words</u> (Old Tappan, New Jersey: The Fleming H. Revell Co., 1966), II, 144.

3   Walter K. Price, <u>Jesus' Prophetic Sermon</u> (Chicago, Illinois: Moody Press, 1972), p. 142.

they will be saved if they are generous and open handed."[4] Two important points need to be noted here. First, those who will receive praise from the Lord for their generosity will respond with an unawareness of their own actions. Therefore, they obviously did not show their generosity in order to obtain this reward. Secondly, the Lord does not say that those on the left never showed generosity. He said that inasmuch as they had not shown generosity to the least of these they had not shown it to Him.

The difference between the judgments of the two groups is essentially the same as between being under "grace" as opposed to being under "law." Under the grace of God, the righteousness of Jesus Christ is imputed to the believer by faith, thereby making the works performed by the believer the result of being in right relationship with God. To one who places his or her faith in Jesus Christ, good works are not done in order to please or gain favor with God, for the purpose of earning salvation, rather they are done, because God works within the believer both to will and do of His good pleasure (Philippians 2:13; Ephesians 2:10). Through faith in Jesus Christ, the believer is declared righteous before God. Righteousness, on the other hand, cannot be obtained through the law (Galatians 2:21; 3:11). Those who desire to be judged by the law have placed themselves under a curse, because the law requires that they should keep the entirety of the law (Galatians 3:10). Anyone who breaks the smallest point of the law, therefore, is guilty of breaking the whole law (James 2:10). In the same way, those who have not shown their generosity to the least of Jesus' brethren have not shown generosity to Him. Those who refuse to come under the grace of God, by faith in Jesus Christ, remain under the law to be judged according to the law.

---

4   C.H. Spurgeon, <u>Matthew: The Gospel of the Kingdom</u> (Pasadena, Texas: Pilgrim Publications, 1974), p. 230.

In Matthew 25:40, Jesus makes reference to a group which He calls "My brethren." Though it is not essential to understand the identity of this group, in order to understand the judgments taking place, we will briefly examine the possible identities of this group. The word "brethren," appears in Scripture with a variety of meanings. The possibilities include: immediate family members, those belonging to the nation of Israel, Jesus' disciples, member of the Church, or those who hear and do the will of God. The later of these is what Jesus used when He was told that His mother and brothers were looking for Him (Luke 18:19-21). Yet, if this were the meaning which Jesus intended, then He would be including the group which He was addressing, since the sheep would be among those who have heard and done the will of God.

For reasons mentioned earlier, this book has concluded that Jesus did not speak directly concerning the Church during the giving of this discourse. However, there exists the possibility that He could have been speaking of the Church indirectly, in light of the fact that the book of the Revelation speaks of the "armies in heaven" which will follow Him when He comes (Revelation 19:14). A problem still exists in this interpretation, however, since the group which Jesus is addressing is supposed to have shown generosity to the brethren in this context. The Church, however, will have been raptured prior to the tribulation period, making them unavailable for receiving the acts of kindness on the part of the sheep.

The apostles were promised that they would be seated on thrones with Jesus in His Kingdom (Matthew 19:28). Yet their responsibility is given as judging the nation of Israel and those being judged in this scene are the non-Jewish nations. Moreover, the same problems exist with the apostles being the brethren in view here as did with the

Church being recognized as the brethren: the apostles will not be present when the acts of generosity will most likely be performed.

Another possibility is the remnant of Israel which will have been purged in the wilderness upon Christ's return (Ezekiel 20:35-38; Matthew 24:37-41). This would appear to be the most likely of the possibilities. If the brethren are indeed from the nation of Israel, then there is yet another possibility. This could be in reference to the 144,000 witnesses who will stand with Jesus when He returns. John wrote that these would follow Jesus wherever He goes (Revelation 14:1-5). The purged remnant of Israel, however, would constitute an even larger group, which would account for the generosity which Jesus seems to be implying in this description. Whatever the case, the acts of generosity must be viewed as the basis for rewards, not as the basis for receiving eternal life.

In this discourse, Jesus answered the disciples' questions, but He also revealed to the disciples that the most important thing for them to know wasn't the exact timing of His return. The most important thing to know was what their responsibility would be while He was away. The same is true today and will be until He comes. He is coming and that is a certainty, but there is a preparation which must be made for the Kingdom, and we are to be involved in it. The final chapter of this book will review in detail the principles which have been revealed in this significant prophetic discourse. That which Jesus revealed to His disciples on the Mount of Olives, nearly 2,000 years ago, should be of major concern to us today, as we await the soon arrival of the King of kings and Lord of lords.

CHAPTER 18
WATCH AND PRAY

The winding journey up the path of Mount Olivet on that Tuesday of the Passion Week was a thought provoking hike for Jesus' disciples. The events of the morning and the words of the Master had given them much to consider. They had been eagerly anticipating the day when Jesus would claim His rightful place on the throne of David. Yet, they could readily recognize that the religious leaders of Jerusalem were not about to receive Jesus, the Messiah, with open arms. Moreover, Jesus had pronounced desolation upon the city, and had spoken of a complete dismantling of the temple. They must have wondered how all of these things could fit in with the establishment of the Kingdom. They were ready to see Jesus rule and reign over the nation of Israel in His glorious Kingdom, but they were oblivious to the fact that He would, within a few days, be hung on a cross to die for the sins of the world.

Jesus, however, understood His mission. He had come into the world, in order that He could live a sinless life, and then take the penalty of sinners upon Himself. Jesus knew that He had come to Jerusalem to be rejected, falsely accused, scorned, and put to death. He knew this and He had tried to make His disciples understand this, but they could only envision Him as the King upon His throne with them reigning along side of Him. They were looking for their place within the Kingdom of Jesus Christ. So, as they came to a place to rest along the narrow road leading up Olivet, some of them came to Him, privately, and asked the questions, which they had formulated while hiking up the winding path. They wanted to know the signs which would indicate the desolation of Jerusalem, the end of the age, and the time of Jesus' return. The wording of the questions revealed that they had concluded that all three events would take place at nearly the same time, sometime in the immediate future.

As Jesus set forth His reply to these inquiries, He began by taking the focus off of the Kingdom, itself, and placing it on those things which would be of immediate importance to His disciples. He knew that it was important for the disciples to have faith regarding the promise of the Kingdom, but He also knew that the Kingdom would not be established, as they were anticipating, in the immediate future. The disciples needed to realize this, as well, in order to focus on the task which lay before them. The promise is the hope which was set before them, but along with the hope there is a responsibility. These disciples were to be the first to spread the good news of the coming Kingdom throughout the whole world. They would take this news before councils, governors, and kings. In doing so, they would be beaten, imprisoned, and even put to death. Yet the gospel of the Kingdom would be spread throughout the world.

At this point, let us take note that the relationship between the Church and the Kingdom of God is not in view during the presentation of the Olivet Discourse. That relationship is a matter which would require the writing of another entire book. The aspect of the Kingdom which is viewed in the discourse is the earthly Kingdom with Jesus Christ on the throne in the reestablished nation of Israel.

A few commentators have attempted to draw a distinction between the "gospel of the kingdom" and "the gospel of grace," as though the "gospel of the kingdom" somehow belongs strictly to the nation of Israel. E. Schuyler English, for example, identifies the "gospel of the kingdom" with the "Jewish Age," thus making a sharp distinction between it and the gospel belonging to the Church.[1] This separation of gospels, however, is not warranted by Scripture.

The preaching of the good news regarding the Kingdom did not end with the advent of the "Age of Grace." On the day of Pentecost, Peter implicitly preached an offer of the Kingdom in his sermon to the multitudes (Acts 2:14-36). As the Church advanced into Samaria, Philip preached with regard to both "the things concerning the kingdom of God and the name of Jesus Christ" (Acts 8:12). When the apostle Paul spread the gospel to the Gentiles, he did not cease to preach concerning the Kingdom.

On the return portion of his first missionary journey, Paul, along with Barnabas, encouraged the believers and exhorted them, saying, "We must through many tribulations enter the kingdom of God" (Acts 14:22) While witnessing in the synagogue of Ephesus, Paul reasoned and persuaded for three months "concerning the things of the kingdom of God" (Acts 19:8) Paul's parting words to the elders at Ephesus, prior to his return to Jerusalem, were:

> But none of these things move me; nor do I count
> my life dear to myself, so that I may finish my race
> with joy, and the ministry which I received from

---

1   E. Schuyler English, <u>Studies in the Gospel According to Matthew</u> (New York: Our Hope Publications, 1925), pp. 170-173.

the Lord Jesus, *to testify to the gospel of the grace of God*. And indeed, now I know that you all, among whom I have gone *preaching the kingdom of God*, will see my face no more [*italics* this writer's] (Acts 20:24-26).

In the closing chapter of the book Acts, Luke records that Paul was still preaching the kingdom of God (Acts 28:23,31) Paul emphasized the Kingdom in his epistles (Romans 14:7; I Corinthians 4:26, 15:59; Galatians 5:21; Ephesians 5:5, Colossians 1:13, 4:11; I Thessalonians 2:12; II Thessalonians 1:5; II Timothy 4:1,18). Moreover, Paul taught that there was only one gospel (Galatians 1:6-9). For Paul, the preaching of Christ and the preaching of His Kingdom were integrally related.

In addition to these evidences that the "gospel of the kingdom" and the "gospel of grace" are synonymous, Jesus Himself offered the keys to the kingdom to His disciples (Matthew 16:19). The keys which He offered consisted of the statements that He was going to Jerusalem, and that He would be put to death, and that in three days He would rise from the dead (Matthew 16:21). Those keys constitute the grace of God, displayed in the substitutional sacrifice of His Son for the sins of the world, "that whoever believes in Him should not perish but have everlasting life" (John 3:16; I Corinthians 15:1-4; Matthew 16:21). The kingdom of God and the grace of God are integral parts of the same gospel. Both deserve preaching in our world today.

Since Jesus' disciples had connected the demise of Jerusalem with His return, Jesus began this teaching by warning of false messiahs who would come after His departure. The disciples had no idea as to where Jesus was going. Their only thought was that when He returned, then He would establish the promised Kingdom. Jesus realized that, with this anticipation on the part of His disciples, they would be tempted to follow after every rumor of His coming. They would want to be present when Jesus entered the royal city to take His rightful place on David's throne. Therefore, Jesus began by warning them not to go after the rumors of His return.

Jesus gave such a warning twice during the discourse. The first warning was directed to the disciples who were with Him on Olivet. The second warning was given with regard to events which will surround the time period known as the great tribulation. As this age draws to an end, and Jesus' return is about to take place, there will again be false prophets, false messiahs, and rumors of His return. The Antichrist will, at that time, attempt to deceive even the elect, if that were possible. The warning is the same: don't listen to the rumors and don't go where they say the Messiah is waiting. The return of Jesus will not be hidden. When He comes again the whole world will recognize His return.

Jesus' disciples apparently understood that this age will end with God's judgment being poured out. They understood, at least, that the description given by Jesus of the temple's destruction could only take place through deliberate human effort. Wars, famines, pestilences, earthquakes, and other natural disturbances have long been viewed as part of God's judgment upon the world. Jesus, therefore, told His disciples that such upheavals must take place prior to the end, but they in themselves are not the signs of the end. Furthermore, Jesus told the disciples that they should not be troubled with coming wars and rumors of wars. The disciples would have much more pressing matters with which to be concerned.

Things haven't changed much, since the days of the apostles, with regard to the way that wars, rumors of wars, and natural disturbances are viewed. Many begin to look for the end of the age when they hear of such things taking place. Yet, the admonition remains the same today as it was to the disciples. These things must take place, but we are not to let our hearts be troubled by them. They are indications that the time is drawing near for Christ's return, but we are to be occupied with the ministry which Jesus has given us until His return.

Unlike the disciples, as they sat with Jesus on the slope of Olivet, we have been told Jesus will come for His Church before the terrible events of the great tribulation begin. Yet, as we watch the signs of our times, we can see those days approaching rapidly, which means that the day of Christ's return for His Church is approaching even more rapidly. Our hope is to be with our Lord when He comes, and, just as the disciples needed to focus their attention on the responsibility which lay before them, we must do the same. Toward the end of the first century A.D., the apostle John wrote, "And everyone who has this hope purifies himself just as He is pure" (I John 3:3).

Throughout the opening of the discourse, Jesus emphasized that the gospel of the Kingdom must be spread throughout the whole world before His return and the end of the age. Those who were to have the responsibility of spreading that good news were the disciples and those who would follow after them. Jesus told the twelve, when they were first commissioned to preach the gospel of the Kingdom, that they would not "have gone through the cities of Israel before the Son of Man comes" (Matthew 10:23). The commission won't be completely fulfilled until the return of Christ. Part of the responsibility that we, as believers in Jesus Christ, have is to be occupied with the spread of the gospel of the Kingdom. Just prior to Jesus' ascension into heaven, He gave a commission to His disciples and to those who would follow after them. He told them that they were to go, and as they were going, they were to teach all nations, baptizing their disciples in the name of the Father, and the Son, and the Holy Spirit, teaching them whatever Jesus had taught them (Matthew 28:18-20). This is the great commission which is often spoken of in the Church today. Yet, as we consider the words which Jesus gave to the disciples on Olivet, prior to His crucifixion, we see that the commission is the very same, to take the gospel of the Kingdom to all nations. The commission hasn't changed. Believers in Jesus Christ still have the responsibility of making disciples wherever they go.

Not only did Jesus tell His disciples that they would be responsible for spreading the gospel, but He also told them of the things which they would suffer in order to spread the news. There are very few people who can truthfully say that they really enjoy suffering. Yet, joy through suffering is possible. Jesus agonized in the garden of Gethsemane, as He looked to the hour for which He had come. He knew what would take place as He gave up His life on the cross. He was about to take upon Himself the sins of the world. The Father would turn His back on Him. What exactly that meant is beyond our comprehension. Yet, in spite of the suffering, the writer of Hebrews tells us that Jesus endured the cross, counting the shame as nothing, for the joy that was set before Him (Hebrews 12:2). James wrote that we, too, should consider it joy when we encounter various trials, realizing that the end result is our maturity in Christ (James 1:2-4). Perhaps the apostle Paul captured the essence of this joy best when he wrote:

> The Spirit Himself bears witness with our spirit that we are children of God, and if children, then heirs--heirs of God and joint heirs with Christ, if indeed we suffer with Him, that we may also be glorified together, For I consider the sufferings of this present

      time are not worthy to be compared with the glory
      which shall be revealed in us (Romans 8:16-18).

Such joy does not always manifest itself in hilarity and laughter, though it may, but, more often, it manifests itself in a tranquility which comes with the peaceful assurance that, whatever trials may be encountered in serving Jesus Christ, the believer can look toward the certain promises of God.

    As Jesus spoke of the sufferings which the disciples would have to endure in their witness to the Kingdom, He also assured them that, when it came time for them to give testimony before kings, governors, and councils, they would not have to deliberate on their own defense. These men were not highly educated men, learned in the manner of presenting an impressive legal defense; rather they were fishermen and tax collectors. Yet, the testimony which they would give was not to be of their own contrivance. They were to rely on the words given to them, in that hour, by the Holy Spirit. Note that though Jesus told them this, He had not yet revealed to them that they would be indwelt by the Holy Spirit or that they could be filled with the Holy Spirit. That is information which was yet to be unveiled. The responsibility given to the disciples was that of testifying with regard to Jesus Christ, but the ability to do so was to come from the power of the Holy Spirit.

    God calls the follower of Jesus Christ to "be a vessel of honor, sanctified and useful for the Master, prepared for every good work" (II Timothy 2:21). Moreover, the believer is to present his or her "members as instruments of righteousness to God" (Romans 6:13). Those who are in Christ Jesus do not perform good works in order to find favor with God so that they can be saved, rather "we are His workmanship, created in Christ Jesus for good works, which God prepared beforehand that we should walk in them" (Ephesians 2:10). Therefore, we can see that the actual responsibility of the believer is more availability than ability. When the believer becomes available, then God supplies the ability. As the apostle Paul wrote, "I can do all things through Christ who strengthens me" (Philippians 4:13).

Only after Jesus had shown the disciples those things which would be of greater importance, did He tell them of the sign which would indicate the demise of the city of Jerusalem and its temple. He made it perfectly clear that Jerusalem was not the place to be, once the armies were seen surrounding the city. If the disciples had any preconceived notions that they should wait for Jesus' return within the city, during the days surrounding the city's demise, they were dispelled by what Jesus had to say in this portion of the discourse. Furthermore, Jesus indicated that there would be a period of time which would elapse between the fall of the city and His return, when He predicted that, "Jerusalem will be trampled by Gentiles until the times of the Gentiles are fulfilled" (Luke 21:24).

Jesus went on to explain that the end of the age would be characterized by false teachers, betrayals, deceptions, and lawlessness leading to a coldness of heart. The apostle Paul, in writing to the Thessalonians, explained that the mystery of lawlessness was already at work, and that it will abound when the lawless one is revealed (II Thessalonians 2:7-8). Toward the close of the first century A.D., the apostle John wrote that it was the last hour and that many antichrists were already in the world (I John 2:18). Since the beginning of the Church, there have been false teachers, betrayals, deceptions, and lawlessness.

Though Jesus was speaking of events which will take place during the end of the Jewish age, there is a great deal to be learned by the Church in the present time. We are living in a time when lawlessness prevails. There are not enough prisons to hold all of those who have broken the laws of the land. And, beyond that, God's laws are actually being ignored in this land. God holds the sanctity of life as something precious, even from the very moment of conception (Psalm 139:13-16). Man is made in God's image (Genesis 1:27; 9:6). Yet, every day, in this country, we allow the unhindered slaughter of thousands of unborn children. Jesus told His disciples that, because lawlessness would abound, the love of many would grow cold. There is a tendency to become overwhelmed by the onslaught of lawlessness, even to the point of throwing up one's hands in despair, and saying "What's the use? I can't change the world." The truth is, we can't change the world, but Jesus Christ can change the hearts of men and women who are in the world, when we make ourselves available to be used for the furtherance of His Kingdom. Christians, we need to keep our eyes focused on the Lord Jesus Christ, and not on the world. With our eyes upon Jesus, we can be used of Him as having a part in fulfilling His words, "And this gospel of the kingdom will be preached in all the world as a witness to all nations, and then the end will come" (Matthew 24:14)

Once the disciples had an understanding that the end would not come immediately, Jesus was able to proceed with answering the question regarding the signs of the end of the age and His return. Jesus set forth the *abomination of desolation*, spoken of by Daniel the prophet, as the sign which would mark the end of the age. This will be the signal to flee Judea, during the latter days. Jesus noted that the events which will follow this sign will be on a greater scale than anything which has ever occurred in history. The warnings for those living in those days are much the same as those which were given to the disciples themselves. The disturbances in heaven and on earth will strike fear into the hearts of many in those days.

Those who believe in Jesus Christ, during those days, are warned to beware of the rumors of Christ's coming. Jesus says to them that His coming will be as open and visible as the flashing of lightning. Deceptions and treachery will abound in those days. Jesus' return, however, will be marked by a sign which will appear in heaven, and then He Himself will come in the clouds with power and great glory. When He returns, Jesus will no longer be the suffering servant, but He will be the victorious King of kings, and Lord of lords. At that time, Jesus will send His angels to gather the believing remnant of Israel back into the land. The "Kingdom Age" will soon begin.

The middle portion of the discourse was presented in such a way as to give the signs for which the disciples had inquired, while at the same time, without setting an exact time frame for the occurrence of the events. In fact, as Jesus gave the parable concerning the fig tree and the other trees, He stated that only the Father knows the date and the hour of Jesus' return. For this reason, Jesus called for a discernment of the times on the part of all. When He does return, many will be unprepared and many will be taken away in judgment, much as those who perished in the days of Noah. Therefore, Jesus again commanded that those who know these things should watch and pray.

The remainder of the discourse, with the exception of the final scene, consists of a series of parables whose central theme is based on readiness. The principles from these parables are intended for all who will listen to the words of Jesus. In chapters fourteen through sixteen of this book, four such parables are identified. Each parable speaks with regard to the issue of being ready for the coming of the King. Yet, each one has a slightly different emphasis.

The entire discourse seems to have been directed toward these parables. Jesus answered the disciples' questions, but He went a step further in giving the significance behind knowing these things. For those, other than the people who will experience the trials of the great tribulation, a knowledge of end time facts should be more than a mere academic exercise, which it could become, were it not for the fact that there is a responsibility on the part of those who have heard these teachings. This is why the parables are pivotal to understanding the discourse. They teach us what that responsibility is.

The first parable taught in the discourse is that of a master and his doorkeeper. The basic command for this parable is to watch. Just as a doorkeeper has the charge to watch for intruders, those who have heard the words of Jesus have, among other responsibilities, the charge to keep a watch over the teachings of Jesus. In the opening of the discourse and, later, in the section directed toward the tribulation saints, Jesus spoke of false prophets who would deceive many. Throughout the age, there have been false teachers who have twisted the words of Scripture and perverted the meaning intended (II Peter 2:1; 3:16). These have tried to allure, even the elect, away from the truth, but their end is destruction (II Peter 2:18-20). Those who have heard the Truth have a responsibility to keep watch. Moreover, the doorkeeper who fails in his task will not know the day or the hour of his master's return. Jesus commands His servants, therefore, to watch, lest when He comes they may be found sleeping.

For many today, there is so much activity and busy schedules which crowd out time to be alone with Jesus and His Word. Often times, those who lack the time to be with Jesus, rely on others within the body of Christ to do the studying of the Word for them. Rather than study out, for themselves, what the Scriptures teach on an area of concern, they turn to the nearest Christian bookstore and find what someone else has written on the subject. This in itself is not an unhealthy thing to do, but there is a danger of adopting the author's view on the matter without discerning what God had to say on the subject. They trust the author, because the author is "Christian." They may, however, overlook the command to watch. Reading books by Christian authors can be profitable, but it is not a substitution for spending time in the Word of God, the Bible. Unlike the writers of Scripture, the authors of Christian literature are not necessarily inspired by God and are therefore fallible. These writers may have been given divine illumination on a given subject, but, as human beings, each of them is still subject to error. Therefore it is wise to read with a discerning heart and an open Bible.

The apostle Peter counseled that false teachers carouse in their deceptions, while they are among us, and they beguile unstable souls (II Peter 2:13-14). Jude wrote of these impostors that "certain men have crept in unnoticed" (Jude 4). God has placed some within the Church who have been given the task of warning, rebuking, and exhorting the body of Christ (Ephesians 4:11; II Timothy 4:1-5; Titus 2:15), but the responsibility to watch has been given to each individual believer. Jesus said, "And what I say to you, I say to all: Watch_" (Mark 13:37)

The second of the readiness parables takes the relationship between the master and the servant a step beyond the first. In the parable about the faithful and evil servants, Jesus marks the distinction between those who have received Him and those who have made a mere profession of knowing Him. The good and faithful servant is recognized by the fact that, when the master returns, he is found doing the task which the master had given him. This servant was assigned the responsibility of giving food to the household in due season. Likewise, as those within the body of Christ, we have the task of building one another up in the faith. There are a variety of ways in which this task can be accomplished, and, again, the task is to be accomplished in due season. Some have the responsibility of teaching or preaching. Others are evangelists. Still others are involved in encouraging, or helping, or giving, or intercession. Yet, each member of the body has been gifted by the indwelling Holy Spirit to perform one or more tasks of edification within the body. In this way, the individual members of the Church serve the household of Christ in due season.

The evil servant, on the other hand, pretends to be a true servant of the master, but, as time goes by, he begins to show that his heart is not in doing the bidding of the master. First, he begins to beat his fellow servants. Since he has chosen to rebel against his master, and the master is not present, he shows his contempt by striking out against the other servants. When this isn't enough, he turns to the ways of the world, and begins to eat and drink with the drunkards. He deludes himself into believing that God will not see his actions. Yet, he fails to recognize that Christ is coming at a time of which he is not aware. The end appointed to such an individual is weeping and gnashing of teeth: a fate which belongs to the lost.

The churches of our generation have within them professing Christians who are dissatisfied with the work which Christ is doing in the lives of those who have made a personal relationship with Jesus. The problem isn't that the true Christians have neglected their responsibility, but those who haven't yielded their live to Jesus Christ haven't a clue as to what that responsibility is. The result is that these who merely profess to know Jesus begin to hinder the work, rather than edifying the saints. However, as those who know Christ continue to edify one another, the impostors will either come to realize their folly, or eventually they will distance themselves from those who are following Christ. At the close of the first century A.D., the apostle John wrote of such individuals, saying:

> They went out from us, because they were not of us; for if they had been of us, they would have continued with us; but they went out that they might be made manifest, that none of them were of us. (I John 2:19)

With regard to the third readiness parable, it is important to make a distinction between interpretation and application. From the perspective of interpretation, this parable was most likely directed toward those who belong to the nation of Israel during the later part of the time of Jacob's trouble. Nevertheless, regarding application, the principles taught in this parable are applicable to people within the Church today. For the former group the Bridegroom is coming at the close of the great tribulation. As for the latter group, Jesus is coming for His Church prior to the time of the great tribulation. The preparations to meet the Bridegroom apply equally to both groups.

The foolish virgins represent those who think that they are prepared, but have neglected something which they should have known to do. They either expected that others would provide for them, or thought that there would be sufficient time for them to acquire what was needed when the bridegroom arrived. Both assumptions proved to be wrong. Jesus Christ has required but one thing of those who would be prepared for His coming. That is to receive salvation through faith in His finished work. He has completed all other preparations by going to the cross to take upon Himself the penalty for the sins of the whole world (I John 2:2).

Many seek to prepare themselves for meeting their Creator, but fail to acquire the essential ingredient, a personal relationship with Jesus Christ. He alone is the way to salvation, "for there is no other name under heaven given among men by which we must be saved" (Acts 4:12). Faith in Jesus Christ isn't optional for salvation. It is the only way. There is no other. The same is true for those of the nation of Israel who would desire to enter David's royal Kingdom. The only way will be through faith in the King Himself. Those who receive Him will also receive the Kingdom, while those who have neglected to receive Him will be shut out. Jesus had clearly stated that many will come to Him saying that they have done great things in His name, but He will send them away because He never knew them (Matthew 7:21-23). No amount of good works will gain access into the Kingdom. Without a personal relationship with the King, all the good works produced are no better than lamps without oil.

The last of the four parables, once again, is addressed to those who have heard the words of Jesus. Some have heard little, while others have heard much, but each one is responsible for doing something with that which he has heard. The wicked and lazy servant had received a little in comparison to the other servants, but he chose to hide what was entrusted to him. This servant knew what would be expected of him, but he chose to ignore the truth. The end result for him was that he was cast into the outer darkness. He refused the light which had been entrusted to him, so he will receive no more light for all eternity.

To close the discourse, Jesus chose to present a scene which will take place just prior to the establishment of His earthly Kingdom. In this scene, the nations of the world are gathered before Him, and divided with the righteous on His right hand and the wicked on His left. All of the righteous are welcomed into the Kingdom, while the wicked are sent to eternal punishment.

The righteous will not be on the Lord's right hand because they will have been kind or generous. In fact, they will not even be aware of the fact that they will have served the Lord in the manner to which He will speak. They will be there because they will have a personal relationship with the King. The good deeds they have done will have been through this relationship. The wicked, on the other hand, will be punished according to their lack of kindness and generosity. Mind you, Jesus doesn't say that they have never shown kindness or generosity in their lives, but rather, being judged by their works, their works will fall short of completeness.

Those who do not choose salvation in Jesus Christ will be judged according to their works, but man's works fall woefully short of God's expectations. As Isaiah wrote, "But we are all like an unclean thing, and all our righteousnesses are like filthy rags" (Isaiah 64:6). One can either rely on their works or they can receive the righteousness of Jesus Christ by faith in Him, but, in the end, only those who have a relationship with Jesus will enter the Kingdom

Jesus' disciples were anxious to know the signs which would mark the desolation of Jerusalem, the end of the age, and of His return, because they were anticipating an immediate establishment of the Kingdom. Jesus answered their inquiries, but not because the Kingdom was to be established within their lifetimes, but because they needed to understand that to those who have been given the privilege of entering the Kingdom, there has also been given a responsibility. Keeping that responsibility may involve suffering or even death, but the reward outweighs the sufferings. Those who have heard the words of Jesus are responsible for what they have heard. This discourse answers the inquiries of Jesus' closest disciples, but it goes beyond that to explain exactly what the responsibility is to those who have received these words.

Jesus is coming and He brings His reward with Him. Those who are prepared to meet Him shall enter into their reward. Unto those who have heard and failed to prepare, the doors to the Kingdom will be eternally shut. For those who have a personal relationship with the King, let us watch and pray. To those who have not yet committed their lives to Jesus Christ, "Behold now is the accepted time; behold now is the day of salvation" (II Corinthians 6:2). "EVEN SO COME LORD JESUS_" (Revelation 22:20)

Books

Baughman, Ray E. The Life of Christ Visualized. Mesquite, Texas: Shepherd Press, 1968.

Boettner, Loraine. The Millenium. Grand Rapids, Michigan: Baker Book House, 1958.

Edersheim, Alfred. The Life and Times of Jesus the Messiah. 2 Vols. Grand Rapids, Michigan: WM. B. Eerdmans Publishing Company, 1962.

Fox, John. Fox's Book of Martyrs. Edited by William Bryon Forbush. Philadelphia, Pennsylvania: Universal Book and Bible House, 1962.

Gundry, Robert H. The Church and the Tribulation. Grand Rapids, Michigan: Zondervan Publishing House, 1973.

Kik, J. Marcellus. Matthew Twenty-four: An Exposition. Swengal, Pennsylvania: Bible Truth Depot, [n.d.].

McCall, Thomas S. And Levitt, Zola. Satan In the Sanctuary. Chicago, Illinois: Moody Press, 1973.

Price, Walter K. Jesus' Prophetic Sermon. Chicago, Illinois: Moody Press, 1972.

Ramm, Bernard. Protestant Biblical Interpretation. Boston: W. A. Wilde Company, 1950.

Reese, Alexander. The Approaching Advent of Christ. London: Marshal, Morgan and Scott, 1937; reprint International Publishers, 1975.

Commentaries

Alford, Henry. <u>Alford's Greek Testament</u>. 4 Vols. Grand Rapids, Michigan: Guardian Press, 1976.

Alford, Henry. <u>The Greek Testament</u>. 4 Vols. Revised by Everett F. Harrison. Chicago, Illinois: Moody Press, 1958.

English, E. Schuyler. <u>Studies in the Gospel According to Matthew</u>. New York: Fleming H. Revell, 1935.

Godet, Frederick. <u>Commentary on the Gospel of St. Luke</u>. 2 Vols. Translated by M. D. Cusin. Edinburg: T&T Clark, [n.d.].

Leavell, Roland Q. <u>Studies in Matthew: The King and the Kingdom</u>. Nashville, Tennessee: Convention Press, 1962

Lenski, R. C. H. <u>The Interpretation of St. Matthew's Gospel</u>. Minneapolis, Minnesota: Augsburg Publishing House, 1943.

Morgan, G. Campbell. <u>Studies in the Four Gospels</u>. Westwood, New Jersey: Fleming H. Revell Company, 1931.

Spurgeon, C. H. <u>The Gospel of the Kingdom</u>. Pasadena, Texas: Pilgrim Publications, 1974.

Walvoord, John F. Matthew: <u>Thy Kingdom Come</u>. Chicago, Illinois: Moody Press, 1974.

Wuest, Kenneth S. <u>Mark In the Greek New Testament for the English Reader</u>. Grand Rapids, Michigan: Wm. B. Eerdmans Publishing Company, 1949.

Reference Works

Josephus, Flavius. The Works of Flavius Josephus. Translated by William Whiston. New York: A. L. Burt Company, Publishers, [n.d.].

Metzger, Bruce, editor. The Aprocrypha of the Old Testament: Revised Standard Version. New York: Oxford University Press, 1973.

Moulton, Harold K., editor. The Analytical Greek Lexicon Revised. Grand Rapids, Michigan: Zondervan Publishing House, 1977.

Strong's Exhaustive Concordance of the Bible, The Old Time Gospel Hour Edition Lynchburg, Virginia: Dr. Jerry Falwell, director, [n.d.]. Greek Dictionary of the New Testament

Tenney, Merrill C., general editor. The Zondervan Pictorial Encyclopedia of the Bible. 5 Vols. Grand Rapids, Michigan: Zondervan Publishing House, 1976.

Vine, W. E. Expository Dictionary of New Testament Words. Old Tappan, New Jersey: Fleming H. Revell Company, 1966.

MAGAZINE ARTICLES AND UNPUBLISHED WORKS

Toussaint, Stanley. "The Argument of Matthew." Th. D. Dissertation, Dallas Theological Seminary, 1957.

Walvoord, John F. "Christ's Olivet Discourse on the End of the Age." Bibliotheca Sacra. 128 (April, 1971): 109-116.

Walvoord, John F. "Christ's Olivet Discourse on the End of the Age." Bibliotheca Sacra. 128 (October, 1971): 316-326.

Walvoord, John F. "Christ's Olivet Discourse on the End of the Age." <u>Bibliotheca Sacra</u>. 129 (January, 1972): 20-32.